FOLENS IDEAS BANK POETRY

Richard Brown

Contents

The poems listed in a suggested order of difficulty, starting with the least demanding.

How to use this book	2	*The Word Party* by Richard Edwards	26
What is Pink? by Christina G. Rossetti	4	*To Find a Poem* by Robert Fisher	28
Littlemouse by Richard Edwards	6	*The Way Through the Woods* by Rudyard Kipling	30
The Owl and the Pussy-Cat by Edward Lear	8	*First Visit to the Seaside* by Raymond Wilson	32
The Dream of the Cabbage Caterpillars by Libby Houston	10	*Four Children, One Being ...* by Julie Holder	34
Christmas Images by Richard Brown	12	*The Swan* Anon.	36
Divali by David Harmer	14	*Between the Lines* by Ruth Trowbridge	38
Oh, I Wish I'd Looked After Me Teeth by Pam Ayres	16	*Victoria 1837* by Eleanor and Herbert Farjeon	40
Five Haiku by Gina Douthwaite	18	*Wee Jouky Daidles* by James Smith	42
The Marrog by R. C. Scriven	20	*Kubla Khan* by S. T. Coleridge	44
The Letter 'L' Writes a Poem by Richard Brown	22	*Grammar in a Nutshell* Anon.	46
Sea-Fever by John Masefield	24	Eight ways to help ...	48

How to use this book

Ideas Bank books provide you with ready to use, practical photocopiable activity pages for your children **plus** a wealth of ideas for extension and development.

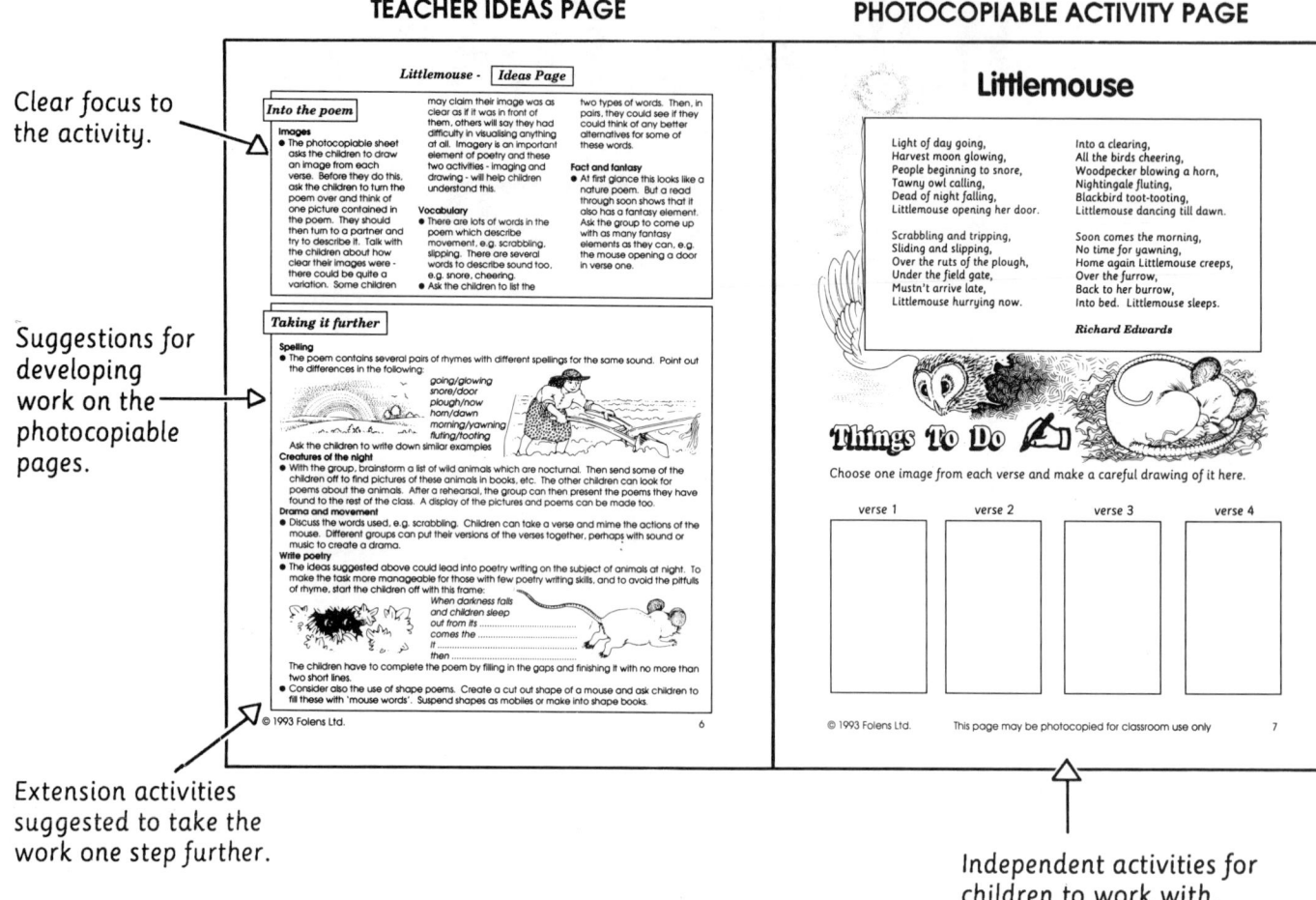

Clear focus to the activity.

Suggestions for developing work on the photocopiable pages.

Extension activities suggested to take the work one step further.

Independent activities for children to work with.

- Time saving, relevant and practical, **Ideas Bank** books ensure that you will always have work ready at hand.

Acknowledgements

Littlemouse and *The Word Party* by Richard Edwards from *The Word Party*, The Lutterworth Press. *The Dream of Cabbage Caterpillars* by Libby Houston by permission of the author. *Divali* by David Harmer by permission of the author. *Oh, I Wish I'd Looked After Me Teeth* by Pam Ayres © the author. *Five Haiku* by Gina Douthwaite by permission of the author. *The Marog* by R C Scriven by permission of the author. *Sea-Fever* by John Masefield. The Society of Authors as the literary representative of the Estate of John Masefield. *To Find a Poem* by Robert Fisher by permission of the author. *First Visit to the Seaside* by Raymond Wilson from *Daft Davy: A Story in Verse*. Faber and Faber Ltd. *Four Children, One Being ...* by Julie Holder from *Between the Lines* by Ruth Trowbridge. Reprinted from *Always Begin Where You Are* ed. W Lamb, McGraw Hill by permission of the National Council of Teachers of English "English Journal" Vol 64 No. 5 (USA) where it first appeared. *Victoria 1837* by E and H Farjeon from *Kings and Queens* by permission of J M Dent & Sons Ltd.

Folens books are protected by international copyright laws. All rights reserved. The copyright of all materials in this book, except where otherwise stated, remains the property of the publisher and author(s). No part of this publication may be reproduced, stored in a retrieval system, or transmitted, in any form or by any means, for whatever purpose, without the written permission of Folens Limited.

Folens do allow photocopying of selected pages of this publication for educational use, providing that this use is within the confines of the purchasing institution. You may make as many copies as you require for classroom use of the pages so marked.

This resource may be used in a variety of ways; however it is not intended that teachers or students should write into the book itself.

© 1993 Folens Limited, on behalf of the author.

Cover by: In Touch Creative Services Ltd.   Illustrations by: Dandi Palmer.   Cover Photo © The Image Bank, Gianalberto Cigolini.

First published 1993 by Folens Limited, Albert House, Apex Business Centre, Boscombe Road, Dunstable, LU5 4RL, England.

ISBN 1 85276532-1   Printed by Ashford Colour Press

Introduction

One of the most exciting developments in recent decades in the world of children's book publishing is the huge increase in the number of books of poetry written mainly for children. On every subject, in every mood, at every level and in every poetic form, poets have created texts for young readers which are as rich and appealing as anything else you will find in picture books and extended narratives. Poetry now constitutes a major source of reading and language development which cannot be ignored or seen as an optional extra.

Poetry is for hearing, for reading together, for re-reading and learning, and for those quiet moments of private reading. It can also take the reader into the whole world of language, spoken, written and graphic; and this is the focus of this book.

The nature of the resource
This resource gives you twenty-two poems to use mainly with children 7-11 years. Each poem is photocopiable for classroom use. This ensures that every child has the opportunity not just to hear a poem being read, but to see how the poet has chosen to arrange it on the page. It allows for simultaneous reading and discussion in paired, group and class contexts. Above all, it allows for the poem to be at the centre of a range of rich language and cross-curricular work.

The choice of poems
The poems have been chosen with a number of criteria in mind to try and ensure a balance of experience:
- a mix of new, familiar and traditional
- some pre-twentieth century poems
- covering a range of poetic styles and techniques
- often challenging in language and concepts, but avoiding the archaic and the obscure
- interesting and relevant to this age group
- with a gender balance in subject
- rich in potential for follow-up language and cross-curricular work
- a few with links to major celebrations, e.g. Divali, Christmas, Guy Fawkes Night.

The poems are ordered roughly into a sequence of difficulty, starting with those more suitable to less experienced readers. However, this order is only a rough guide, since responses to poems can be at several different levels of engagement. You will be the best judge of the suitability of poems for particular pairs and groups.

Organising group reading and follow-up work
One of the main purposes of this resource is to provide you with challenging texts for group reading and associated language work - which will not cost the school a lot to provide. The group needs to be manageable, perhaps no more than ten within it. Ideally, the poem is introduced by you and read with the group. Some initial queries and discussion will follow and then the work suggested at the foot of the poem will be selected, explained and initiated. This will require that the rest of the class are working very quietly on activities which do not need immediate teacher supervision.

If you want to have the whole class working in groups on poems in this way at the same time, you will need to repeat the above with each group. You will probably need to use a different poem, at a different level of difficulty, with each group.

Setting up the work will thus be demanding on you at first, but will then give your class many hours of varied and challenging work in which their language is developed in a variety of ways.

Follow-up ideas: the pupil's sheet
Each poem usually has two follow-up ideas at the foot of the page. These give the suggestions for some initial work around the poem. Their purpose is to ensure that pupils engage with the poem in a number of ways, re-reading, questioning, speculating, developing understanding of vocabulary, form and content. Sometimes the ideas are presented as a straight choice; sometimes one is linked to the other.

The class sharing one poem
You may judge that the levels of reading and understanding in your class are such as to enable you to select one poem to use with the whole class. Many poems have such a wide appeal that this is possible (although you will ensure that if there are pupils in your class who need a lot more support than their peers, this is planned for).

You can read the poem aloud to the class first, then give out copies to the pupils for a re-reading, followed by an initial discussion. The class can then move into pairs or groups to begin the follow-up work as appropriate.

Follow-up ideas: the teacher's page
You may decide that the activities on the pupil's page will be sufficient for your purpose. It is worth examining the ideas on the teacher's page, however, to see the potential for learning that the poem, in addition, presents.

The ideas are divided into two sections: **Into the poem** and **Taking it further**.

Into the poem provides a number of ideas for exploring the poem itself. These will often include developing discussion around the poem's content and the vocabulary; and studying the poetic techniques and forms used.

Taking it further lists a number of associated ideas which use the poem as a stimulus for general English work (such as further reading, spelling and handwriting) and cross-curricular work. This often includes writing and art; it sometimes includes subjects such as science, music, history, RE, book-making and mini-projects.

Linking the poem with the wider curriculum
As a matter of course, many of you will want to integrate work on the poems into a project or area of study in planning or in operation. For example, you will probably want to use **The Marrog** as part of a space project; **Sea-Fever** and **First Visit to the Seaside** as part of a study of the sea or a topic on water. **Wee Jouky Daidles** will fit into a study of language variation; and **Divali**, **Christmas Images** and **Five Haiku** at the appropriate seasonal time.

It makes sense to do this because the children will be more receptive to the poem's content and theme.

© 1993 Folens Ltd.

What is Pink? - Ideas Page

Into the poem

Techniques of poetry
- The form of this poem has four aspects which you could point out to the children:
  - the first line about each colour consists of a question and an answer
  - the second line tells you more about the answer
  - every other line repeats the phrase, 'What is ...'
  - pairs of lines rhyme.

Description
- Ask the children to turn over the poem. Then ask them to describe a picture which illustrates the poem. This can be through talk and by choice through writing. Let them refer to the poem again if necessary. It is an activity which helps the children to recall visual images and to realise how central to poetry imagery is.

Taking it further

Punctuation
- Use the questions and answers in the poem to discuss dialogue and the punctuation of speech. Write out the poem correctly punctuated as dialogue. What differences are there between both versions? Which is the better?

Writing poetry
- Ask children to take a colour and use it as the title of a poem. Each line can start with a repetition, e.g. 'Red is ...' or it can simply be a list of things associated with that colour. Once the first draft is done, help the children to make their list visually sharper and more interesting, e.g. the line 'Red is a beach ball' can become 'Red is a beach ball floating out on the tide,' or 'Red is a huge, bouncing beach ball'.
- The children could write a simplified, non-rhyming version of the Rossetti poem using the question and answer structure,
  e.g. 'What is turquoise?
     The glint on a fish's scale.
     What is black?
     A night without a moon ...'
- You could give the children a list of colours not included in the Rossetti poem, asking them not to attempt to rhyme. What other words have no rhymes?
- For children who find the concept of rhyme quite difficult, try simple rhyme games, e.g. rhyme tennis. One child says one word - pink - to another. The partner has to rhyme this - brink - and will score for this. The game continues until someone cannot think of a rhyme the winner starts again using a new word. The winner starts again using a new word. Game, set and match!
- Discuss the spelling of different rhymes and why certain words sound the same but are spelt very differently, e.g. white, light.

Art
The poem would make a good subject for a collage.
- Ask the children to work in fours.
- Give three of them paper and scissors and ask them to draw and colour the objects in the poem: a pink rose, a fountain, a red poppy, a swan, yellow pears and an orange.
- The fourth person should prepare the background on a large sheet of paper, to include barley, clouds in a blue sky (some of them violet), a pond, lake or river, grass and a twilight sun. Once everything is ready the group discuss the best arrangement of the objects on the background before sticking them down.
- Display the collage alongside a handwritten copy of the poem.

© 1993 Folens Ltd.

What is Pink?

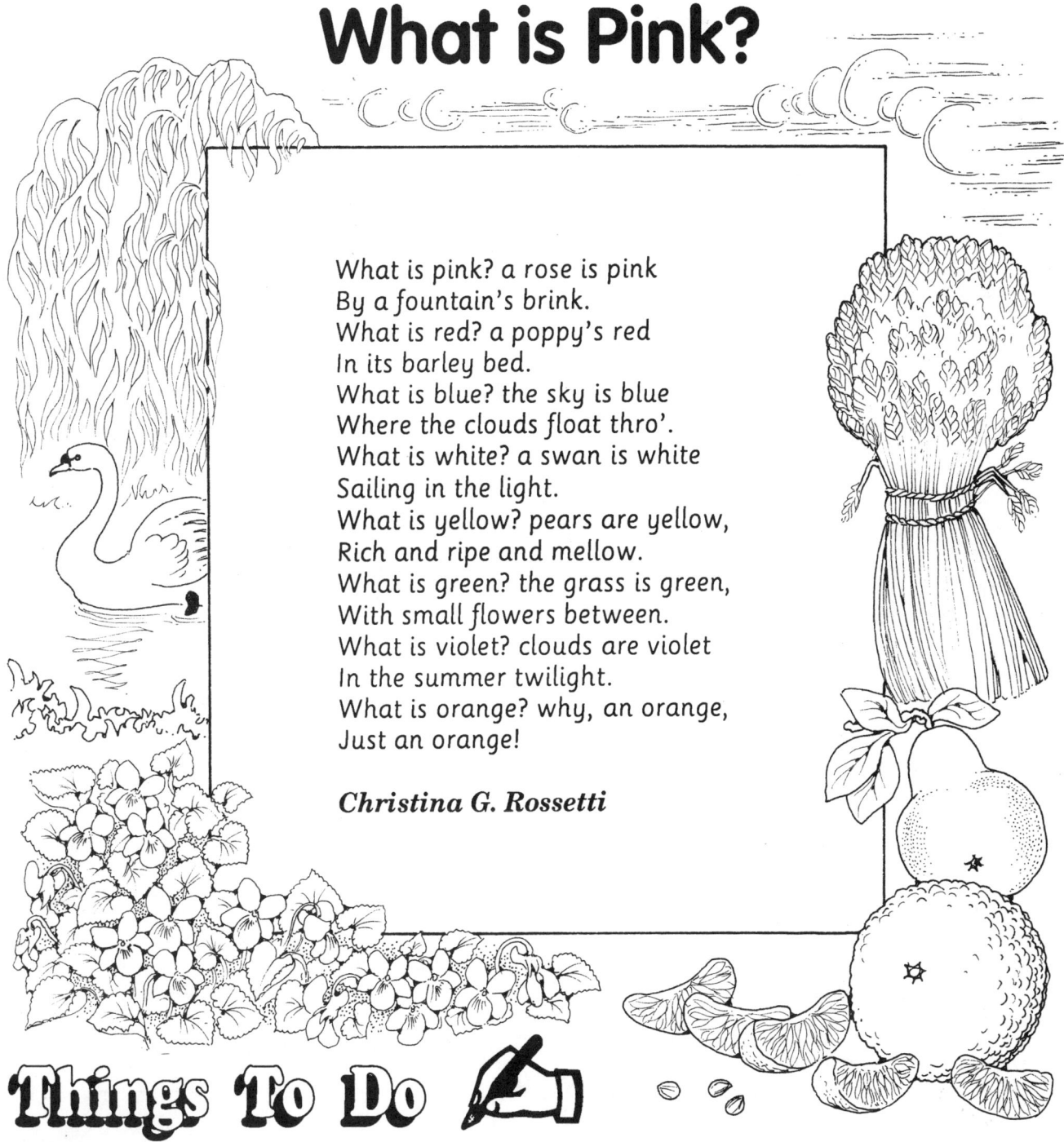

What is pink? a rose is pink
By a fountain's brink.
What is red? a poppy's red
In its barley bed.
What is blue? the sky is blue
Where the clouds float thro'.
What is white? a swan is white
Sailing in the light.
What is yellow? pears are yellow,
Rich and ripe and mellow.
What is green? the grass is green,
With small flowers between.
What is violet? clouds are violet
In the summer twilight.
What is orange? why, an orange,
Just an orange!

Christina G. Rossetti

Things To Do

- In pairs, read this aloud. One of you asks the questions. The other gives the answers. Then talk about the poem's title. Can you think of a better one?

- In pairs, think of up to five things for each colour. For example, What is red? a ripe tomato, a fire engine, blood, etc. Try to find things which are always the same colour, e.g. the word 'socks' could have been in the red list, but that breaks the rules because they don't have to be red.

- Write a colour poem using words in your list.

Littlemouse - Ideas Page

Into the poem

Images
- The photocopiable sheet asks the children to draw an image from each verse. Before they do this, ask the children to turn the poem over and think of one picture contained in the poem. They should then turn to a partner and try to describe it. Talk with the children about how clear their images were - there could be quite a variation. Some children may claim their image was as clear as if it was in front of them, others will say they had difficulty in visualising anything at all. Imagery is an important element of poetry and these two activities - imaging and drawing - will help children understand this.

Vocabulary
- There are lots of words in the poem which describe movement, e.g. scrabbling, slipping. There are several words to describe sound too, e.g. snore, cheering.
- Ask the children to list the two types of words. Then, in pairs, they could see if they could think of any better alternatives for some of these words.

Fact and fantasy
- At first glance this looks like a nature poem. But a read through soon shows that it also has a fantasy element. Ask the group to come up with as many fantasy elements as they can, e.g. the mouse opening a door in verse one.

Taking it further

Spelling
- The poem contains several pairs of rhymes with different spellings for the same sound. Point out the differences in the following:

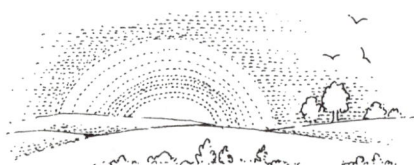

going/glowing
snore/door
plough/now
horn/dawn
morning/yawning
fluting/tooting

Ask the children to write down similar examples

Creatures of the night
- With the group, brainstorm a list of wild animals which are nocturnal. Then send some of the children off to find pictures of these animals in books, etc. The other children can look for poems about the animals. After a rehearsal, the group can then present the poems they have found to the rest of the class. A display of the pictures and poems can be made too.

Drama and movement
- Discuss the words used, e.g. scrabbling. Children can take a verse and mime the actions of the mouse. Different groups can put their versions of the verses together, perhaps with sound or music to create a drama.

Write poetry
- The ideas suggested above could lead into poetry writing on the subject of animals at night. To make the task more manageable for those with few poetry writing skills, and to avoid the pitfulls of rhyme, start the children off with this frame:

*When darkness falls
and children sleep
out from its ....
comes the ....
It ....
then ....*

The children have to complete the poem by filling in the gaps and finishing it with no more than two short lines.

- Consider also the use of shape poems. Create a cut out shape of a mouse and ask children to fill these with 'mouse words'. Suspend shapes as mobiles or make into shape books.

© 1993 Folens Ltd.

Littlemouse

Light of day going,
Harvest moon glowing,
People beginning to snore,
Tawny owl calling,
Dead of night falling,
Littlemouse opening her door.

Scrabbling and tripping,
Sliding and slipping,
Over the ruts of the plough,
Under the field gate,
Mustn't arrive late,
Littlemouse hurrying now.

Into a clearing,
All the birds cheering,
Woodpecker blowing a horn,
Nightingale fluting,
Blackbird toot-tooting,
Littlemouse dancing till dawn.

Soon comes the morning,
No time for yawning,
Home again Littlemouse creeps,
Over the furrow,
Back to her burrow,
Into bed. Littlemouse sleeps.

Richard Edwards

Things To Do

Choose one image from each verse and make a careful drawing of it here.

verse 1	verse 2	verse 3	verse 4

The Owl and the Pussy-Cat - Ideas Page

Into the poem

Discussion
- To help the children explore what is happening in this poem, you could ask them to speculate in discussion around the following questions:
  - What did the pea-green boat look like?
  - What might have happened before the start of the poem which made the Owl and the Pussy-Cat take to sea?
  - What sort of things might have happened to the two during the year and a day they spent at sea?
  - What might a bong-tree look like?
  - What might have happened to the two after they were married?
  - Is this just a nonsense poem written for fun, or is it in fact a love poem in disguise?
  - Why should anyone choose to write a nonsense poem?

Techniques of poetry
- This is a highly patterned and very skilfully formed poem. Once the children have explored the meaning of the poem, you could move on to point out some of the features of its form. For example:
  - the verses each consist of two quatrains, (i.e. four line rhyming verses) with a repetitive refrain added
  - there are eight examples of internal rhyme, (i.e. a rhyme within the same line):
    verse 1: *honey/money*
    verse 2: *married/tarried, away/day, wood/stood*
    verse 3: *willing/shilling, away/day, mince/quince, hand/sand.*
    Practise some of these simple techniques
  - repetition of rhythm and form is used in the last four lines of each verse to act as a refrain.
- Display the poem - poster-size if possible - on a pinboard and ask the children to write what the poem makes them think and feel. These can be copied on to large speech bubbles cut out from paper and displayed around the poem.

Taking it further

Illustrations
- There have been several picture book or illustrated versions of this poem. Ask a few children to make a search in the school for the poem and share with the children the different approaches taken.

Nonsense poems
- The poem may well stimulate an interest in Lear's nonsense verse. Share with the class some other Lear classics, e.g. **The Jumblies, The Dong with a Luminous Nose, The Pobble Who Has No Toes**, and so on. Collected editions of Lear's nonsense poems are easily available. You could then go on to look at the work of present day writers of nonsense poetry for children such as Spike Milligan, Colin West and Shel Silverstein.

Puppetry
- If you are planning puppet making with the children, some of them could make the characters in this poem and use the puppets as part of a performance of the poem with younger children.

Art
- The poem could act as a stimulus to picture making of various kinds. Give the children the option of making a picture of :
  - a pea-green boat
  - the Owl singing with his guitar
  - a bong-tree
  - Piggy-wig
  - the turkey
  - mince, quince and the runcible spoon (they do exist!)
  - the Owl and the Pussy-Cat dancing by the light of the moon.
- The pictures could be displayed, captioned by appropriate lines from the poem.

Music
- The poem is very musical and in the first verse the Owl sings a song.
- Identify the musical elements - long sounds - 'beautiful', the rhythm and repetition.
- Encourage groups of children to set the poem to music. There will be two separate tunes within the poem: one for the verse and one for the refrain. Rehearse on audio tape and perform.

© 1993 Folens Ltd.

The Owl and the Pussy-Cat

This is a very well-known nonsense rhyme written in 1868.

The Owl and the Pussy-Cat went to sea
   In a beautiful pea-green boat:
They took some honey, and plenty of money
   Wrapped up in a five pound note.
The Owl looked up to the stars above,
   And sang to a small guitar,
'O lovely Pussy, O Pussy, my love
   What a beautiful Pussy you are,
            You are,
            You are,
   What a beautiful Pussy you are!'

Pussy said to the Owl, 'You elegant fowl,
   How charmingly sweet you sing!
Oh, let us be married; too long have we tarried,
   But what shall we do for a ring?'
They sailed away, for a year and a day,
   To the land where the bong-tree grows;
And there in a wood a Piggy-wig stood,
   With a ring at the end of his nose,
            His nose,
            His nose,
   With a ring at the end of his nose.

'Dear Pig, are you willing to sell for one shilling
   Your ring?' Said the Piggy, 'I will.'
So they took it away, and were married next day
   By the turkey who lives on the hill.
They dined on mince and slices of quince
   Which they ate with a runcible spoon;
And hand in hand, on the edge of the sand,
   They danced by the light of the moon,
            The moon,
            The moon,
   They danced by the light of the moon.

Edward Lear

Things To Do

- In groups of four, practise reading this poem aloud. One of you should be the poet, one the Owl, one the Pussy-Cat and one the Pig. Record your reading on audio tape. Listen carefully to see whether you can improve on your performance and share your reading of the poem with an audience.

- Draw a pictureof the Owl and the Pussy-Cat in their pea-green boat. Give each a speech bubble in which you write the words they are saying in the poem.

The Dream of the Cabbage Caterpillars - *Ideas Page*

Into the poem

Sequencing
- Ask pairs to cut one of their copies of the poem into the six verses. Is it at all possible to rearrange the order of the verses without losing the sense of the poem? In doing this the children will have an added purpose for reading the poem intensively.

Book making
- Provide each pair with two plain sheets of A4 paper. These should be folded into two to make an eight-page booklet which can be stapled. A verse should be written on each of the inside pages leaving space for an illustration. The cover can be designed and an explanatory blurb written for the back.

Techniques of poetry
- At a later stage point out to the group how this poem illustrates some of the basic elements of poetic form.
- Ask simple questions to get children to realise that poets write in a particular way to achieve certain effects.
  - How many lines are there in every verse?
  - Which lines rhyme? Which words rhyme?
  - Some lines do not have any punctuation at the end. Why do you think this might be?
  - Do all lines in poems have to have punctuation at the end of them?
  - What kinds of punctuation can you find in the poem?
  - Draw a line down the left-hand side of the poem following the outline of the verses. What do you notice? Why do you think the poet chose to do this?

quatrains: *four line rhyming verse*
indentation: *every second and fourth line is indented: does this have any affect on the reader?*
rhyme: *a pattern of rhyming pairs at the end of the second and fourth lines*
enjambement: *the sense of one line (or verse) running on into the next*
repetition of certain sounds, *e.g. dreamed/beam/roamed/changed and more obviously the many words ending in -ing.*

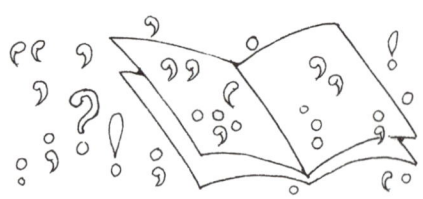

Taking it further

Spelling and handwriting
- Ask the children to pick out all the words ending with -ing, then write them in their best joined handwriting from memory. Those who finish before the others can be asked to find other -ing words to add to the list.

Science
- The poem is a poet's view of the caterpillar's metamorphosis into a butterfly. Use it alongside nature work on this subject: as part of a display, topic file, and presentations.

Art
- The poem could lead into a study of the patterns to be found on butterfly's wings. These make a marvellous stimulus for pattern work, observational drawings, paintings and mobiles.

Writing: comparing genres
- Reproduce a piece of prose from an information book which describes the change from caterpillar to butterfly. Make sure the reading level is appropriate for the group. Then ask the group to contrast it with the poem, saying what the essential differences are, not just in terms of form, but also in the overall effect on the reader.

Writing poetry
- The children could write poems based upon their observations of caterpillars and butterflies (or pictures of them).
  More ambitiously, some could write a poem in dialogue form, a caterpillar and a butterfly talking about their differences and how they feel about them.

© 1993 Folens Ltd.

The Dream of the Cabbage Caterpillars

This is a poem about how a caterpillar changes into a white butterfly.

There was no magic spell:
   all of us, sleeping,
dreamt the same dream - a dream
   that's ours for keeping.

In sunbeam or dripping rain,
   sister by brother
we once roamed with glee
   the leaves that our mother

laid us and left us on,
   browsing our fill
of green cabbage, fresh cabbage,
   thick cabbage, until

in the hammocks we hung
   from the garden wall
came sleep, and the dream
   that changed us all -

we had left our soft bodies,
   the munching, the crawling,
to skim through the clear air
   like white petals falling!

Just so, so we woke -
   so to skip high as towers,
and dip now to sweet fuel
   from trembling bright flowers.

Libby Houston

Things To Do

- Talk with a partner or your group about what is happening to the caterpillar in each verse. You may find it helpful to refer to science information books on the subject.

- Try writing a two-column poem. The right-hand column lists what a caterpillar is and the left-hand column lists what a butterfly is. Like this:

Caterpillar is
green or striped
round and wriggly
hairy ...

Butterfly is
patterned
light and fragile
smooth as silk ...

Christmas Images - Ideas Page

Into the poem

Exploring feelings about Christmas
- Christmas is an emotional high-point for most children and it is worth using the occasion to explore their feelings about it and at the same time developing a vocabulary for the expression of feelings. The first activity on the pupil's page encourages children to recall images of past Christmases. Some of these can be shared with the group and the class. The poem contains negative as well as positive feelings. Point this out to the children and then begin to list in two columns - positive feelings and negative feelings - words which sum up the feelings of the children as they recall images of their own Christmases.

Techniques of poetry: acrostic and haiku
This poem makes use of two well-known poetic forms: acrostic and haiku.
The acrostic form is pointed out on the pupil's page and is relatively easy for young children to grasp. The haiku is less obvious and if the children have not yet learnt about it, this poem can be the vehicle for introducing it.
- Ask the children: how many lines in each verse?
  how many syllables in each line? (explain what a syllable is if they do not know)
  what pattern does each verse follow?
- It is helpful to count syllables in words. Try with the children's own names. They will see that their names will contain different numbers of syllables and will also develop a different sense of rhythm. Ray - mond Bar - ker is very different from Al - ex - an - der Firth. A classroom display could be created showing the differences in numbers of syllables. More work on haiku and syllables can be found on page 18.
- Older children might be able to develop rhythms of all the names into a class rap!

Taking it further

Poetry writing: acrostic and haiku
- Having encountered the acrostic form, you can encourage the children to use it to write Christmas poems. Subjects could be anything to do with the season, e.g. presents, pudding, turkey, baubles, tinsel, stockings, cards, carols, church-going, etc.
- Acrostics around the word 'Christmas' can also be written and copied into cards made by the children to give to family, friends and relatives.
- Similarly, you can get them to experiment with the haiku, writing one or two from a similar list of items. The more successful haikus could be copied out in a large script - or wordprocessed - and be used as part of a Christmas display.
- Cut out Christmas shapes and make poems into Christmas mobiles or hang them individually on the school Christmas tree.

History
- Make the poetry the centre of a display about Christmases of the past. Victorian Christmas is an easy one to focus on. Research into the history of the Christmas tree and into Dickens and the kinds of Christmas people were meant to have then. Is this a true representation of what life was like?
- Look at Christmas in other countries and their beliefs. Why do certain countries not believe in St. Nicholas?
- Link in with other Festivals of Light at the same time of year - Divali, Hannukah. Why do people celebrate these?

Resources

Poems about Christmas
Probably the best collection of Christmas poems for children is:
The Oxford Book of Christmas Poems edited by Harrison and Stuart-Clark, Oxford University Press 1983 ISBN 0-19-276051-3.
It is worth seeking out this wonderful collection and sharing some of the poems with your class.
Also, John Foster's collection **Let's Celebrate**, Oxford University Press 1989 ISBN 0-19-276085-8 has some Christmas poems in it.

© 1993 Folens Ltd.

Christmas Images

What images do you remember of Christmas?

Crackers glitter in
miniature on the tree, their
secrets kept hidden.

High on the tree-top
the blowsy fairy dreams of
older Christmases.

Reels of parcel tape
soon hang from the dustbin
like a tattered flag.

In the dawn darkness
I felt the mysteries of
my bulky stocking.

Sweets are offered once
more; I can't refuse even
though I'll surely burst.

The time to open
presents never comes, does it?
Then - over, in a flash.

Mince pies are so hot
they burn my tongue. And I'm told
'There, serves you right, see!'

Afternoon: excitement
falls flat, the Queen smiles, and I
whisper, 'Is that all?'

Snowflakes fall at last
and we all stand in the frost
watching in silence.

Richard Brown

Things To Do

- The poem is made up of pictures or images of a child's Christmas. Tell a partner in turn what pictures you recall of your Christmas.

- If you take the first letter of each verse it spells CHRISTMAS. See if you and your partner can think of three things linked to Christmas for each letter, e.g. for the letter C you could have candles, cake and cards. Use these to write your own Christmas poem.

Divali - Ideas Page

Into the poem

Research into the poem's subject: Lakshmi
- It is best to use this poem during the festival of Divali in November. Do some research yourself into the nature and role of Lakshmi in Hindu mythology. Pictures of the goddess will help the children to visualise her. You will be in a better position, then, to help the children understand the note that precedes the poem and to help them carry out activities.

Techniques of poetry
- Point out to the children that this is an example of a free verse poem which sets its own rules: each verse has three lines and the lines are brief. The free verse form is apt here because it represents **the movement of a person's thoughts** at a particular time and place.

Simile
- The poem opens and closes with the same simile. Remind the children of what a simile is - the comparison of one thing with another to bring out a particular meaning or mood - and that it is always introduced with the words 'as' or 'like'.
- Practise using simile. Give groups of children the same statement - it was as clear as ... he jumped like ... and ask them to think of as many comparisons for it as possible. Test them out on the rest of the class. Talk about why some are not as successful as others.
- Consider some simile which have become cliche, e.g. as dead as a door nail. Do children know what these mean? Why do people still use them?
- The poem is in first person and is addressed to the subject of the poem, Lakshmi: **'I will light my lamp for you/Lakshmi ...'** This is a form much used in certain kinds of religious writing such as in prayer which this poem resembles. It appears to be only indirectly addressed to the reader who becomes in effect an eaves-dropper. But this is of course only a device and it is one you can get the children to think about by asking them the following questions:
  - Is the 'I' of the poem David Harmer (the poet) or someone else?
  - If the 'I' of the poem is someone else, who could it be?
  - Do we have to believe in Lakshmi to really like and understand this poem?

Taking it further

Religious education
- The theme of 'light' is central to many religions. This poem gives just one example of its symbolic value. If you have children in your class who practise forms of religion, explore with them what forms the presence of light takes in their religion, e.g. candles, lamps, Christmas and Divali lights, stained-glass windows, and so on. Make some of these symbolic objects with the class.

Poetry writing
- Take 'light' as the theme of the poetry. It can be a free verse with the title **What light means to me**. Or it can be a list of the ways we see light, e.g. dawn, rainbows, reflections, ripples and dapples of light, starlight, moonlight, sunlight, flames, torches, etc. and can have the title **The way I see light**. Or it can be expressed in the negative form, each line beginning with the phrase
  **'No light
  I cannot see the
  ....'**

Art and Craft
- Ask the children to make a house two-dimensionally using thin card or thick paper. It should have plenty of windows with shutters that can be opened. Stick paper on the back of the picture so that when the shutters are opened blazing lamps can be drawn in each window.
- Make shadow puppets and produce a shadow play to tell the story of the Ramayana.

Background

In the autumn the festival of Divali is celebrated by Hindus all over the world. Two Hindus gods, husband and wife Rama and Sita, in the story called The Ramayana, returned to their kingdom much welcomed after fourteen years of exile. Divali celebrates that return.

© 1993 Folens Ltd.

Divali

During Divali, Hindus also remember the goddess Lakshmi, the wife of the great god Vishnu. She represents love, beauty and prosperity. Some Hindus welcome her into their homes with colourful paintings and rows of lamps. It is said that she will not visit houses that are not lit up.

Winter stalks us
like a leopard in the mountains
scenting prey.

It grows dark,
bare trees stick black bars
across the moon's silver eye.

I will light my lamp for you
Lakshmi,
drive away the darkness.

Welcome you into my home
Lakshmi,
beckon you from every window

With light that blazes
out like flames
across the sombre sky.

Certain houses
crouch in shadow, do not hear
your gentle voice.

Will not feel
your gentle heartbeat
bring prosperity and fortune.

Darkness hunts them
like a leopard in the mountains
stalking prey.

David Harmer

Things To Do

- See what you can find out about the goddess Lakshmi. If you are a Hindu yourself, talk to your family about her. If you are not a Hindu but know someone of that religion, ask them about Lakshmi. Write down all that you have learnt and shape it into a poem.
- The poem begins with a comparison called a simile:

    Winter stalks us
    like a leopard in the mountains
    scenting prey.

Can you think of other ways of describing the coming of winter? Complete this in your own way (and do more than one if you like):

   Winter stalks us like ....

Oh, I Wish I'd Looked After Me Teeth - Ideas Page

Into the poem

Pronunciation and colloquialisms

- If you can get hold of a recording of Pam Ayres reciting this poem, the children will be better able to appreciate the hints at pronunciation in the poem, mainly signalled by the dropping of the 'g' in the words ending with the suffix '-ing'. You could discuss colloquial turns of phrase which give it its personal tone, e.g. 'To pass up gobstoppers/From respect to me choppers ...' Get children to record their own versions talking about how it sounds to others.

Personal stories

- Encourage the children to tell each other their experiences of visits to the dentist. For some it could be a subject for writing. What advice would they give to someone who is going to the dentist for the first time?

Limericks

- The verse form of this poem is that of the limerick and the jaunty rhythm and regular rhyme scheme go a long way to making it successful.
- Identify what makes the limerick a specific comic poetic form by reading out other limericks.
- Children can beat out the rhythm and realise the number of stresses in each line.
- Mark out the stresses in a written version, which will also enable you to point out the rhyme scheme.

There **was** a young **lady** from **Crete**,
With **two** very **large** flat **feet**.
When she **hopped** on a **bus**
There was **no** room for **us**,
Her **feet** took up **every** spare **seat**.

- Children can take the first line of famous limericks and write their own versions

Taking it further

Media education 1: an advice leaflet on dental care

- On the pupil's sheet the children are asked to form groups and role-play as advertising agencies and they are asked to produce an advice leaflet. The leaflet could be an A4 sheet folded into three. Show some examples of the format, talk about typography and illustrations, how each of the six panels can have a different focus. Books on dental health will be needed as a reference by the groups. The leaflets, if successful, could then be used to inform other children in the school about dental hygiene.

Media education 2: a fifteen second TV advertisement

- This could develop from the poster or leaflet work suggested on the photocopiable sheet. Small groups of children role-play as rival advertising firms. They each have to supply ideas to the client (i.e. the teacher or another group) for a fifteen second television advertisement for a toothpaste made especially for children. It could star the person saying the poem. Supply each group with some storyboard sheets, i.e. containing boxes of sketches of scenes and lines underneath each box for explanatory captions, and ask the group to use this to plan the advertisement. These are then submitted with a presentation to the client who chooses the one considered the most persuasive.

Health education: dental care

- This poem provides an obvious opportunity to instruct children in dental hygiene. Use posters readily available which shows the best ways of brushing teeth and talk about the creation of plaque which follows from eating sugary foods. Then ask the children to write a letter to the person saying the poem, giving advice on looking after teeth.

Art: make a picture book of the poem

- Form groups of eight and give each child in the group one of the verses to illustrate on pieces of paper, roughly postcard size. These can be mounted in a book with the relevant verse written underneath. The books then become part of the class's reading resource.

© 1993 Folens Ltd.

Oh, I Wish I'd Looked After Me Teeth

Oh, I wish I'd looked after me teeth,
   And spotted the perils beneath,
All the toffees I chewed,
   And the sweet sticky food,
Oh, I wish I'd looked after me teeth.

I wish I'd been that much more willin'
   When I had more tooth there than fillin'
To pass up gobstoppers,
   From respect to me choppers,
And to buy something else with me shillin'.

When I think of the lollies I licked,
   And the liquorice allsorts I picked,
Sherbet dabs, big and little,
   All that hard peanut brittle,
My conscience gets horribly pricked.

My mother, she told me no end,
   'If you got a tooth, you got a friend.'
I was young then, and careless,
   My toothbrush was hairless,
I never had much time to spend.

Oh I showed them the toothpaste all right,
   I flashed it about late at night,
But up-and-down brushin'
And pokin' and fussin'
   Didn't seem worth the time - I could bite!

If I'd known I was paving the way
   To cavities, caps and decay,
The murder of fillin's
   Injections and drillin's,
I'd have thrown all me sherbet away.

So I lay in the old dentist's chair,
   And I gaze up his nose in despair,
And his drill it do whine,
   In these molars of mine.
'Two amalgam,' he'll say, 'four in there.'

How I laughed at my mother's false teeth,
   As they foamed in the waters beneath.
But now comes the reckonin'
   It's me they are beckonin'
Oh, I wish I'd looked after me teeth.

Pam Ayres

Things To Do

- Talk in your group about these questions:
  - is this a funny or serious poem?
  - what do you think your dentist would say about this poem?
  - do you believe what the poet says in verse 6?
  - why do you think the author wrote this poem?
  - is there a message in this poem for you?

- You have been hired to make a leaflet warning children against eating too many sweet things and not brushing their teeth. What will your leaflet look like? What advice will it give? Will it's tone be funny or serious? Think about these three questions, then make a rough plan for your leaflet before you start.

© 1993 Folens Ltd.   This page may be photocopied for classroom use only

Five Haiku - Ideas Page

Into the poem

- Encourage the group to tell each other what happened to them on an occasion when fireworks were present. Then ask each one to describe either a special moment or a favourite firework they enjoyed on the night. You could do this before the children encounter the poem. Alternatively, you could read the poem together, then have the discussion, then return to the poem for a closer reading.

Techniques of poetry

- As the title makes clear, the form of each verse is a haiku. A haiku is a brief seventeen syllable (5-7-5), three line poem which has been popular in Japan for several centuries. Haikus usually stand on their own but, as in the example here, they can form part of a longer poem. Use these points to explain the poem's title. Work on syllables is also to be found on page 12.
- Metaphor is one of the most important devices available to poets. This poem is rich in metaphor and can be used to help children explore how it works. With the children, underline the following metaphors and talk about the meanings they bring to the poem. In the process, search for alternative words and phrases which are not metaphors and then ask what effect is lost in the substitution.

  Metaphors: **Verse 1:** *tantrums, throats,* **Verse 2:** *bones, startled, skull-eyed,*
  Verse 3: *grey veils, black walls,* **Verse 4:** *spear out, webs of wire weaponry, anxious,*
  Verse 5: *stage-struck, signs off.*

- For children who find the concept of comparison without - the use of the word 'like' or 'as' - difficult, ask a series of structured questions which focus on the words:
  - What is a tantrum?
  - Why is the poet using this word to describe a firework?
  - What does a firework remind you of when it is just starting to explode?
  - Do fireworks have throats?
  - What is the poet doing when he gives the fireworks human characteristics?

Taking it further

Writing haikus

- Once children understand the strict syllabic form of the haiku, they can have a go at writing one or two themselves. The subject can be something they remember from fireworks. Remind them of the form: five syllables in line one, seven in lines two and five in line three. The first two lines are usually descriptive, evoking an image and perhaps a feeling or mood too, and the last line usually provides a reflection or comment on the image to give it a deeper resonance. Gina Douthwaite in Five Haiku has not followed this latter point mainly because she is using the haiku here as part of a larger poem with a different purpose. Children enjoy the puzzle-like aspect of the form, they appreciate its brevity, and the discipline it brings helps to sharpen their imagery and choice of words.
- Put each word in a haiku on to an A4 piece of paper. Ask children to create concrete versions of the haiku by each holding the words in the correct order. Replace some of the words with others and discuss the differences, put lines in different orders - what is the effect?

Art: a zig-zag book

- Over a period of time the children can use this poem to build up a small zig-zag book with ten pages. A verse from the poem, carefully copied in best handwriting, calligraphy or on a wordprocessor, alternates with an illustration of that verse. If the task is too demanding or time consuming for some children, it can be shared with one or two others.

History

- As the children to research and write a short account - for a real or imaginary foreign visitor - of the reasons why Bonfire Night is held.

© 1993 Folens Ltd.

Five Haiku

Each verse describes a scene: the fireworks, a bonfire, the smoke, the brief bursts of light in the sky. Don't worry about the title - you'll learn more about that later.

Tantrums of flame gush
from throats of gunpowder tubes.
Take notice of me!

Bones of bonfire shift.
Startled sparks light up skull-eyed
faces in the bushes.

Wisp of grey veil floats,
like some weary Guy Fawkes' ghost,
out through the night's black walls.

Spent sparklers spear out
in webs of wire weaponry
at anxious ankles.

High over midnight
an insistent arc of stars,
still stage-struck, signs off.

Gino Douthwaite

Things To Do

- Underline any words or lines in this poem which you are not sure about. Then talk together about what is happening in each verse.

- Make a list of all the fireworks you saw on Bonfire Night. Then choose five of them and write a sentence about each describing what they looked like once lit.

- When you have finished, have you written a poem?

The Marrog - Ideas Page

Into the poem

Discussion
- Discuss with the children whether they think that (a) within the terms of fiction, there really is a Marrog in the class, or (b) a child in class is daydreaming that he or she is a Marrog. If they think on balance that it is (b), does it make any difference to our understanding of the poem?
- Ask the children to speculate on why they think the Marrog is sitting in a classroom on Earth. What is its purpose?
- Ask the children why they think this can be called a science-fiction poem. What other science fiction have they encountered in books, TV and film?
- Tease out some characteristics of science fiction: invented worlds, draws on technology, set in the future, set in space, etc.

Techniques of poetry
- At first glance this poem resembles a free verse form. However, it has a pronounced rhythm for the first eight lines and a rather complicated rhyming structure. Work out with the children which lines have four beats, which have three and which have two. Underline in colour where the beat is and say the lines together with a pronounced rhythm. Then look at the rhyming words: can the children find a pattern or is it irregular? Underline the pairs of rhymes in different colours. If they had to split the poem into verses, where would they make the breaks?

Taking it further

Writing
- Ask the children to cut out the picture they have made of the Marrog and stick it in the middle of a much large piece of paper. The children can then surround the picture with arrows pointing to various features of the Marrog and explanatory captions saying what the function of each part is. For example, an arrow pointing to the three eyes in the back of the head could be accompanied with a caption which reads: 'On Mars everyone walks backwards, thus eyes are always positioned at the back of the head. The middle eye is for seeing ahead, the other two for seeing left and right.'
- Ask the children to write a story which explains why the Marrog has come to Earth; it can end with the creature sitting at the back of the class.
- Ask the children to write a playscript for two. It consists of the Marrog sending messages back to Mars about his experiences in the school and Mars' puzzled replies.
- Give simple instructions or descriptions to a Martian:
  - How could you instruct a Martian how to make a telephone call if he/she had never made one before?
  - How would a Martian describe a dog?

> Marrog on earth calling Mars ... I have met a creature on four legs which pants a great deal and sniffs me. His teeth and hair suggest he is aggressive. Send back instructions ...

- Write a story about the problems a Marrog would have in your school for a day.

Art
- Groups could make a large collage of the Marrog:
  - in the school environment
  - back home on Mars.

Science and Geography
- Pairs or groups could use techniques developed in these subjects to write a report on the Marrog, in the language of research, which describes its:
  - habitat
  - food
  - habits
  - beliefs
  - problems.
- Children can extend their work on the poem into research into the solar system.
- Imagine the Marrog is planning a holiday somewhere in the solar system - Pluto, Venus, the Moon. What does he/she need to know about the planets to make his trip a happy one?

© 1993 Folens Ltd.

The Marrog

This is a funny science-fiction poem. Read it through carefully.

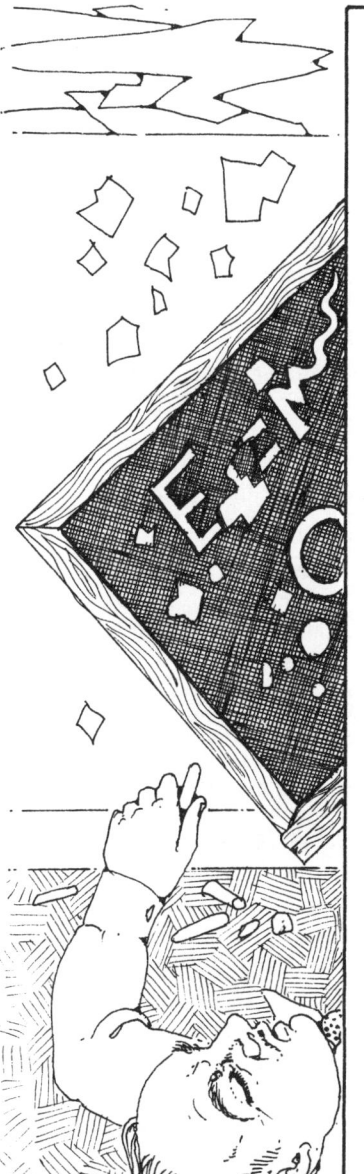

My desk's at the back of the class
And nobody nobody knows
I'm a Marrog from Mars
With a body of brass
And seventeen fingers and toes.
Wouldn't they shriek if they knew
I've three eyes at the back of my head
And my hair is bright purple
My nose is deep blue
And my teeth are half yellow half red?
My five arms are silver with knives on them sharper than spears.
I could go back right now if I liked -
And return in a million light years.
I could gobble them all for
I'm seven feet tall
And I'm breathing green flames from my ears.
Wouldn't they yell if they knew
If they guessed that a Marrog was here?
Ha-ha they haven't a clue -
Or wouldn't they tremble with fear.
Look, look, a Marrog
They'd all scream and shout.
The blackboard would fall and the ceiling would crack
And the teacher would faint I suppose.
But I grin to myself sitting right at the back
And nobody nobody knows.

R.C. Scriven

Things To Do

- Draw and colour a picture of the Marrog, making sure it is exactly as described in the poem.
- Pretend that the Marrog makes himself visible. The teacher faints. The children scatter. The headteacher arrives and tries to talk to the Marrog. In pairs, one of you role plays the Marrog, the other the headteacher. What do you say to each other?

The Letter 'L' Writes a Poem - Ideas Page

Into the poem

Dictionary practise
- In the 'Things to do' section of the pupil's page is a list of words which appear in the poem but which are not likely to be in the everyday vocabulary of the children. More able and experienced children will not need much supervision for this task, but the less experienced will need to work as a group with you. You could compile a glossary of the words with them, referring to a variety of dictionaries.

Vocabulary
- Once you and the children have compiled a glossary of the words, the next step is to see if particular synonyms can be used in the poem to replace the ones in the list. Give the children a further copy of the poem, having first blocked out the words in the list. Ask the children to fill in the gaps using synonyms from the glossary. You can use the terms 'glossary' and 'synonym' during these two activities to introduce the terms in an appropriate context.

Characters
- The poem is about two children. Speculate with your group about these two children, e.g.
    - how old might they be?
    - what might they look like?
    - what sort of place might they live in?
    - what might their families be like?
    - will either of the characters' daydreams, as expressed in the poem, be realised?
- Once you have had this discussion, you could ask the children to draw a picture of Lizzy and Larry, complete with speech bubbles containing the words they say in the poem. If the pictures were clear enough, they could be used as a picture quiz, i.e. another child could be asked to find as many things as they can in one of the pictures beginning with the letter 'l'.

Taking it further

- Children can usually put words in alphabetical order according to the first letter. If all the words in a list start with the same letter, what do they do? Practise this important skill by putting the 'L' words on the pupil page into alphabetical order having to use the second and the third letters of the words.
- As the title of the poem suggests, the stimulus for this poem was in fact the letter 'l'. The challenge was to see if a good poem could be written under such an artificial constraint. The same challenge could be set for the children. Give them the option of writing it in pairs and encourage them to use a dictionary. The poem can be very short, and the only two rules are that it must be interesting and it must make sense.
- These sorts of poems are an extreme forms of **alliteration**, i.e. using a string of words beginning with the same sound. This term can be introduced to the children, and the poems they write could be called 'Alliteration Poems'. There after, when alliteration is encountered in the poems you share with these children, you can point out its use and effect.
- Many children will know tongue-twisters - 'Peter Piper picked a peck of pickled pepper,' etc. Share them with the class and make a collection of them in alphabetical order. These could be collected into a book or made into a class display.

The TV reader test
- Explain to children that when an announcer is interviewed for a job at a TV station he/she has to take part in a test. This involves reading a tongue-twisting passage within a time limit, making as few mistakes as possible. Using the following passage, hold such a competition. Time the competitors and count mistakes made. Can anybody say the passage without any mistakes?

    I bought a batch of baking powder and baked a batch of biscuits. I brought a big basket of biscuits back to the bakery and baked a basket of big biscuits. Then I took the big basket of biscuits and the basket of big biscuits and mixed the big biscuits with the basket of biscuits that was next to the big basket and put a bunch of biscuits from the basket into a box.

© 1993 Folens Ltd.

The Letter 'L' Writes a Poem

Languid Lizzy Lightfoot
lingered last night by a lampost on Lambden Lane
licking a large lemon lolly,
her long lanky legs limp from lack of walking.

A loud, lumpen lout of a lad
- name of Larry Lockbreaker -
with a leer and a laugh said,
'Hey, Lizzy, give us a lick of your lemon lolly.'

Now no love was felt by Lizzy for Larry,
so looking lofty Lizzy said,
'Leave off, Larry, you limp lump,'
and she laughed like a lynx,
leaving Larry looking lost.

But Larry,
lazily licking a length of liquorice,
was less easily lampooned.
He thought, 'You laugh now,
but in time, Lizzy Lightfoot,
(light of my life),
you'll get to like me,
you'll get to love me,
you'll even get to live with me,
and there'll be lots of little Lawbreakers
larking about here, you'll see.'

Little did Larry know that Lizzy
looked on him as a listless loafer.
She was planning to live in London
in a large mansion with luscent chandeliers,
lads in livery bringing letters of love ...

'LIZZY,' came a loud shout down the lane.
'LARRY,' came a ludicrous echo.
Lad and lass slouched into Eleven and Eleven A,
and all that was left in the lamplight
was a lemon lolly stick and a lump of chewed liquorice.

Richard Brown

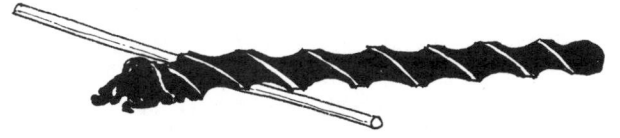

Things To Do

- All the following words appear in the poem. If you are not sure what they mean, check them in a good dictionary:

languid	lingered
lumpen	lounged
lofty	lynx
larking	lampooned
ludicrous	listless
loafer	luscent
livery	

- Did the poet get too carried away with his Ls? Look at each word beginning with L and discuss with a partner whether, if you took out that word, the poem would be better or worse.

Sea-Fever - Ideas Page

Into the poem

Explore the poem
- Write the word SEA in the centre of a large sheet of paper. Ask the group to choose words from the poem which show all the different aspects of the sea the poet likes, e.g. 'the wind's song', 'the white sail's shaking'. Write these around the word SEA in a spider chart form. Or, if you prefer, pairs of children could do this first then share with the group what they have done.
- Speculate with the children on why the poet called this poem **Sea-Fever**.

Techniques of poetry
- The rolling rhythm of this poem is one of its chief attractions. It is based on a pattern of four stresses in each line, e.g.

    I **MUST** go down to the **SEAS** again, to the **LONELY** sea and **SKY**,
    And **ALL** I ask is a **TALL** ship and a **STAR** to steer her **BY** ...

    Point this out to the children, then together say the poem, overstressing the pattern in order that it be understood.
    Does the regular stress suggest the gentle rocking of a boat on the sea?
- The poem is full of alliteration, e.g. the 'w' and 's' sound in

    And the **w**heel'**s** kick and the **w**ind'**s s**ong and the **w**hite **s**ail'**s s**haking.

    Explain to the children the technique of alliteration - a device rarely used outside poetry, tongue-twisters and advertising slogans - then ask them to underline them in the poem using different colours for different sounds. Share the results.
- Develop work on the sounds of words from the use of alliteration. Let children identify soft sounds such as the **wh, sh, ss** words and hard sounds such as '**kick**', '**pick**' in the poem. Look at the line:

    And the **flung spray** and the **blown spume**, and the **sea-gulls crying**

    letting the children note how the **f** and **sp**, the **bl** and **sp** sounds do physically create the spray and its violence. In this way, children can come to realise that poets choose words for a purpose, for their sound value.
- Get groups of children to list hard and soft words to do with the sea - use a thesaurus. Different groups can then write their own poems choosing one mood of the sea, selecting words that they think sound right for that mood. Moods can range from calm to storm - the most important idea is that children are using appropriate sounding words for the creation of atmosphere.

Taking it further

Further reading
- Ask the children to find some other poems about the sea. An anthology of these could be compiled, with each child copying out one of the poems in their best handwriting. Alternatively, a display of the poems could be made for the class to enjoy. Have a read-around session with children volunteering to read one of the poems aloud.

Art
- This poem would make a good stimulus for a sea painting. Show the children different pictures of the sea, discussing how the artist has achieved an effective representation of it.
- Create the character of the person speaking. This is a good opportunity to introduce the idea of the first person narrator in the poem. What do the children think he looks like?
  Draw the character, place him against the sea background produced previously and give him/her a speech bubble containing the child's favourite line from the poem.

© 1993 Folens Ltd.

Sea-Fever

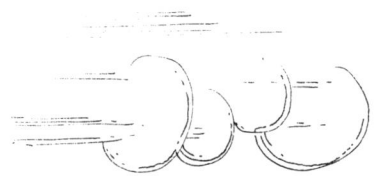
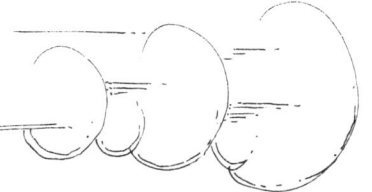

I must go down to the seas again, to the lonely sea and sky,
And all I ask is a tall ship and a star to steer her by,
And the wheel's kick and the wind's song and the white sail's shaking,
And a grey mist on the sea's face and a grey dawn breaking.

I must go down to the seas again, for the call of the running tide
Is a wild call and a clear call that may not be denied;
And all I ask is a windy day with the white clouds flying,
And the flung spray and the blown spume, and the sea-gulls crying.

I must go down to the seas again, to the vagrant gypsy life,
To the gull's way and the whale's way where the wind's like a whetted
knife;

And all I ask is a merry yarn from a laughing fellow-rover,
And quiet sleep and a sweet dream when the long trick's over.

John Masefield

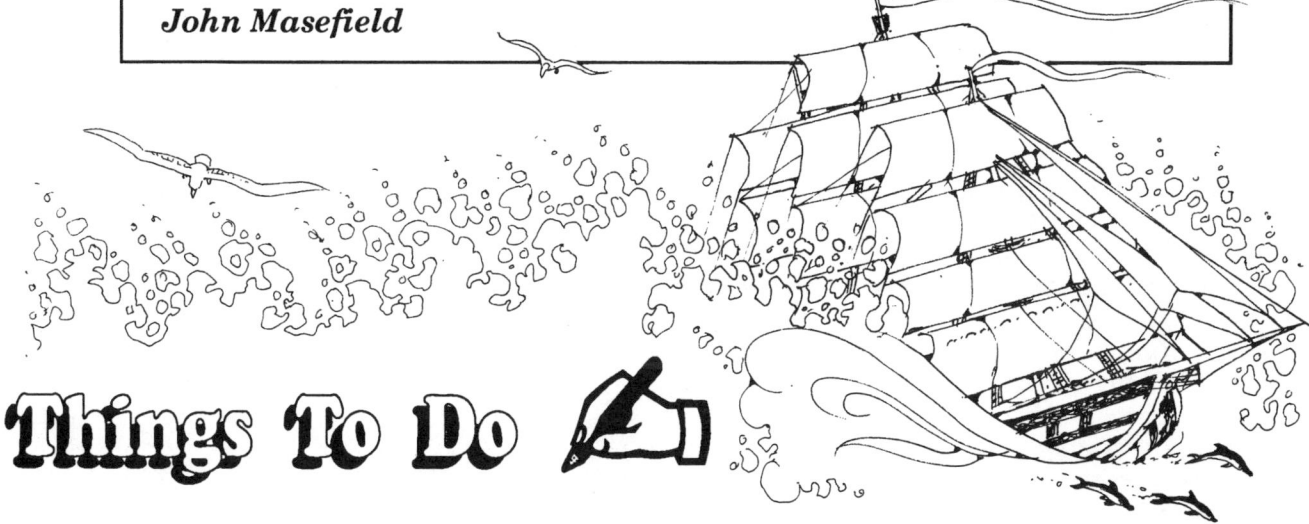

Things To Do

- Many people who learnt this poem by heart as children still remember it and get great pleasure from saying it to themselves. It is a lovely poem to learn. Read it aloud together several times. Gradually you will find you can remember it.

- Draw three postcard-size boxes horizontally on paper. Cut out the verses of this poem and stick them under the boxes in the right order. Now illustrate each verse in the boxes you have drawn.

© 1993 Folens Ltd.   This page may be photocopied for classroom use only

The Word Party - Ideas Page

Into the poem

Discussion
- Ask the children to explain the thinking behind some of the less obvious lines:
  - 'Why do loving words clutch roses?'
  - 'Why are sly words dressed up as foxes?'
  - 'Why do hard words stare each other out?' etc.

Vocabulary
- This poem is an ideal stimulus to developing knowledge of words.
- With the whole group, ask for examples of 'loving words', e.g. love, gentle, close, Valentine cards, kisses, cuddle, etc. Write these words around the stimulus word in front of the children.
- Make this an opportunity to use the Thesaurus and develop knowledge of synonyms. Make games of the word searches
  - How many words with the same meaning can you find?
  - How many words with the same meaning can you find in ten minutes?
- Now give each pair of children one of the following to do the same with: words which are sly, complicated, hard, foreign, careless, long, silly, hyphenated, strong, sweet, kind.
- These could be typed out under their headings on the wordprocessor by some of the children and made into a classroom word book to which new entries can be added as they arise.

Taking it further

Art: cartoons
- Explain to the children that each one of them will be given a line from the poem to illustrate in the style of a cartoon.
- Have some examples of cartoons in comics and cartoon books and discuss these with the children, concentrating on the technique of the medium.
- Then let each child draw a rough for the cartoon. These should be discussed by some of the group as well as by the teacher.
- The finished cartoon with their captions could be mounted into a book - a photo album with cellophane covered pages might be suitable for this.

Poetry writing
- The form of this poem could be adapted to write a poem about people rather than words. The children substitute the word 'faces' for 'words' and change the rest of the line, e.g.

  'Loving faces break into smiles,
  Rude faces look at you sideways,
  Short faces have bigger ears ...'

- Point out to the children that they do not have to use rhyme. You might also want to omit the following: common, swear, foreign, hypenated; and you may want to add some more adjectives of your own.

The feeling of words
- Produce calligrams with the children - poems that visually represent an idea.
  - Long words could be written as if stretched out
  - Loving words as if composed of hearts
  - Strong words as if muscular.

- To help children read more carefully, let them devise memory games to do with the subject matter of the poem.
  - What do careless words do?
  - Which words suck their thumbs?
- Rewrite the first lines of the poem using opposites. Again the Thesaurus would be useful.
  - Hating words clutch black darts
  - Polite words wear nice clothes.

© 1993 Folens Ltd.

The Word Party

Loving words clutch crimson roses,
Rude words sniff and pick their noses,
Sly words come dressed up as foxes,
Short words stand on cardboard boxes,
Common words tell jokes and gabble,
Complicated words play Scrabble,
Swear words stamp around and shout,
Hard words stare each other out,
Foreign words look lost and shrug,
Careless words trip on the rug,
Long words slouch with stooping shoulders,
Code words carry secret folders,
Silly words flick rubber bands,
Hyphenated words hold hands,
Strong words show off, bending metal,
Sweet words call each other 'petal',
Small words yawn and suck their thumbs
Till at last the morning comes.
Kind words give out farewell posies ...

Snap! The dictionary closes.

Richard Edwards

Things To Do

- Read the poem aloud in your group. One person in the group reads the first two words and the rest complete the line. All the group say the last three lines together.

- Next, play this guessing game. Form a group of five or six. One person in the group keeps the score, times the answers and acts as a referee. In turn, each member of the group has to get up and mime one of the lines in the poem. The rest of the group have to guess within fifteen seconds which line it is. The person who gets it right gains two points. If no one gets it right within the fifteen seconds the one who did the mime gains five points. Play until all the lines have been guessed.

To Find a Poem - Ideas Page

Into the poem

Techniques of poetry

- There are three aspects to the form of this poem which it is worth pointing out to the children to help them understand its intentions. The first is that it is written in the form of **advice** given by the poet to the reader (who is understood to be learning the craft of poetry writing). The second is that it is written in a conversational **free verse** form that seems appropriate to the giving of advice. The third point is the hardest to grasp, yet it gets to the heart of the poem. The poet is using what is called a **conceit**. The conceit here is that poems are live beings inhabiting the natural landscape, elusive and fragile things that the reader is advised to track down and capture. Normally we would say that as a poet considers his or her subject, the words form in the mind to invoke it. In this poem, **in order to express the idea that the poet's words and subject can merge and appear indistinguishable**, he uses this novel and effective conceit. To help the children appreciate this device, ask them to discuss the following question:

   'Does the poet actually find poems in nature or just imagine that they are there?'

   Then follow up with:

   'If he knows the poems are only in his imagination, what advice is he trying to give us in this poem?'

Punctuation

- The punctuation in this poem is minimal and appears idiosyncratic. Discuss with the group how the addition of commas, full-stops and capital letters could make the reading of this poem easier for those coming to it for the first time. If you like, you can ask the children to put in the new punctuation as it is discussed.

Taking it further

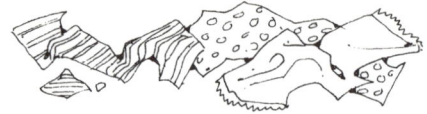

Transformations

- All the images in the poem are from nature. This might suggest to the children that the inspiration for the best poetry comes from nature. To widen this view to include other forms of inspiration, challenge pairs or the group to change the images to urban ones, e.g.

   To find a poem
   listen to the train
   thundering words strange and rare
   look under bins
   there you might find the discarded
   sweet-wrapper of a poem ...

- Encourage the children to keep a poetry notebook for a week and talk about the things they have noticed.
- Help children to value their notebooks by developing their ideas into poems. The poems, their drafts and the original notes can be displayed together to show how the poem was written.

Art and Words

- Ask the children to do a large picture illustrating the poem. Then ask them to write quotations from the poem on to slips of paper and stick them on the picture in the appropriate places.

Resources

- There is a growing body of poetry about the act of writing poetry, some giving insights into the process itself, some wry comments about its difficulties and pleasures, others giving advice.
- As the children will be encouraged to write quite a lot of poetry during their school careers, it is worth sharing some of these poems with them.
- You will find some in the following collections of poetry:

McCORD, David:
   Mr Bidery's Spidery Garden Harrap 1972/ Puffin 1989

STYLES, Morag (ed.):
   You'll Love this Stuff. Cambridge University Press

HARRISON, M. & Stuart-Clark, C. (ed.): *Writing Poems* Oxford 1985

© 1993 Folens Ltd.

To Find a Poem

To be able to write a good poem you need to know a lot more than simply being able to write. You need to be very aware of what you can see, feel, taste, hear and smell. You need to be at least half aware of what is hidden, of mysteries and secrets. The following poem is about how you can find poems anywhere if you know how to look for them.

> To find a poem
> listen to the wind
> whispering words strange and rare
> look under stones
> there you might find the fossil
> shape of an old poem.
> They turn up anywhere
> in the most unexpected places
> look for words that are trapped
> in the branches of trees
> in the wings of birds
> in rockpools by the sea.
> And if you find one
> handle it carefully
> like an injured bird
> for a poem can die
> or slip through the fingers
> like a live eel
> and be lost in the stream.
> Follow whatever footprints are there
> even if no-one else can see them
> for clues to lost poems
> are waiting to be found
> round the next corner
> or before you right now.
> You may have just missed one
> never mind
> look again tomorrow
> you many find your poem
> or your poem
> lost somewhere in the dark
> may be waiting for you.
>
> *Robert Fisher*

Things To Do

- The poem opens with these three lines:
   > To find a poem
   > listen to the wind
   > whispering words strange and rare ...

  On a piece of paper draw wavy lines and swirls in crayon, pastel or coloured pencil to represent the wind. Then write in between and on these lines any words you think are 'strange and rare'. You can find ideas for these words from anywhere you like, e.g. another poetry book, a story, a dictionary, a thesaurus.

- See if you can rewrite all or part of this poem in the shape of a word picture. For example, the wind, a tree, a bird, footprints.

The Way Through the Woods - Ideas Page

Into the poem

Critical reading
Write the following questions on separate pieces of card and use them to help explore the meaning of the poem through group discussion.
- How would the poet have known there was once a road through the wood seventy years ago? If he only imagined that the road had been there, would it make any difference to the poem?
- What reasons could there be for closing the road and planting trees in its place?
- What makes us think the horse and the woman beside it might be ghosts?

Repetition
- Repetition of words, lines and phrases is a key element in many poems.
- In this poem the phrase 'road through the woods' occurs five times. Ask the children to find each use of this phrase.
- Discuss other times in conversation when repetition occurs. What is the effect of this?
- Ask them to speculate on the effect of the repetition in the poem on them as readers. Why is this different than other kinds of repetition?

Vocabulary
- To help the children consider the ingredients of this poem, ask them to sort the following words from it into three groups: **animals/time/rural landscapes.**

seventy	badgers
trees	heath
otters	trout-ringed
evening	pools
coppice	woods
late	horse
anemones	old
ring-dove	

- More mature writers can think of their own words for these three categories and write a three verse poem entitled, 'My Way Through The Woods'.

Taking it further

Write a group poem
- Ask the children to recall a trip to a wood. What pictures come into their minds? Jot down the better of their suggestions in a list in front of them on a large piece of paper or on the board. Choose the best lines and write it out as a list poem. Or ask the children to do this individually. It could then be written out neatly in the children's best handwriting.

Sequence a poem
- Each child should have a copy of the list poem described above. Ask them to cut each line into a strip. They should then resequence it in the way they like best, and then compare their sequence with others. The result could be copied out or stuck on to a sheet of paper. This activity will help them to think about the structure and cohesion of a poem, the way one image follows and links with another.

Art
- The poem is full of rich images. Ask the children to select one detail from it, e.g.
  - the thin anemones,
  - the trout-ringed pools.
This becomes the subject of their picture - which could be a miniature. Alternatively, they could make a landscape showing the wood or how the wood used to look when it had a road running through it.

Onomatopoeia
- There are two examples of this in the poems - swish and whistle, where the sound of the word echoes the sense of the word. Children will be much more familiar with this poetic technique through advertising where it is used more aggressively - **Snap! Wham! Crackle!**
Ask them to list sound words they know. They can then draw the words as calligrams to show how vital they are. Lists can be developed into sound poems: Pop goes the cork flying out the bottle.
Children enjoy making up new onomatopoeic words. What does a word like **flunge** describe?

© 1993 Folens Ltd.

The Way Through the Woods

They shut the road through the woods
Seventy years ago.
Weather and rain have undone it again,
And now you would never know
There was once a road through the woods
Before they planted the trees.
It is underneath the coppice and heath
And the thin anemones.
Only the keeper sees
That, where the ring-dove broods,
And the badgers roll at ease,
There was once a road through the woods.

Yet, if you enter the woods
Of a summer evening late,
When the night-air cools on the trout-ringed pools
Where the otter whistles his mate,
(They fear not men in the woods,
Because they see so few.)
You will hear the beat of a horse's feet,
And the swish of a skirt in the dew,
Steadily cantering through
The misty solitudes,
As though they perfectly knew
The old lost road through the woods ...
But there is no road through the woods.

Rudyard Kipling

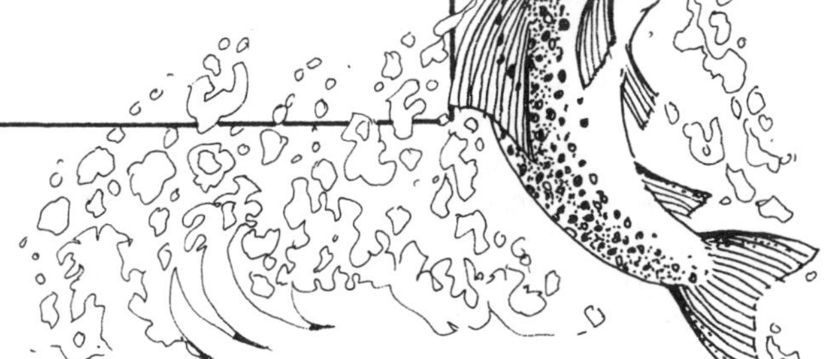

Things To Do

- There are some beautiful lines in this poem. Which lines do you like best?
- What do you think this poem is about? It could be about any of these:
    - woodlands
    - ghosts
    - time passing
    - wildlife
    - the keeper remembers
    - solitude
- Talk about each one. Then choose one you think best sums up what the poem is about. Share your reasons with the group.

First Visit to the Seaside - Ideas Page

Into the poem

Imagery

This poem is rich in images; it does not tell a story but relies on a sequence of carefully wrought pictures to build up a magical sense of a child's first visit to the seaside. To help the children to reflect on some of the imagery, ask them to:
- Underline favourite lines or 'word pictures' in the poem and then share these with the rest of the group.
- Having read and talked initially about the poem, ask the children to turn the poem over and recall one or two images from it. They can describe to the group their image or, if you prefer, they can describe it to a partner.

Personal storytelling
- If some of the group have visited the seaside recently, or can recall a visit, ask them to tell a partner or the group about it. As a follow-up, you can ask them to compare their recollections with the poet's.

Techniques of poetry
- Ask the children to speculate on why they think the poem has three clearly defined parts. Point out the oval shape of the first and last verses: what might the author's intentions be here?
- The poem has an interesting regular rhyming sequence. Ask the children to work out what it is (i.e. first and last verse: aabccbaa; other three verses: abaab).
- The poet make use of alliteration, e.g.
    'Sky and silver sand and shimmering sea'
    'wavelets that withdrew'
    'It was magic and music and motion'

See how many other examples the children can find and ask them why they think the poet has chosen to use alliteration.

Taking it further

Vocabulary
- The poem contains eight hyphenated words and provides an opportunity for a discussion of 'double-barrelled' words.
- The first half of the hyphenated pair qualifies the second half.
- To help the children understand this, ask them to read only the second part of the hyphenated words within their lines in order to illustrate the purpose of the first half. Can the children think of any other hyphenated words?

Art
- Give the children a choice of illustrating one of the verses of the poem in a painting or pastel. Have some examples of seaside paintings to discuss and for the children to study.

Writing
- Using the three starting points of I saw, I heard, I did, children can write shape poems on subjects appropriate to the seaside:
    - Beach balls
    - Buckets
    - Ice-cream
    - Waves.
  Each child can produce one and they can be assembled to create a collage.
- If visits to the seaside are fairly common in class, give the children an opportunity to write:
- a true-life story set at the seaside;
- a poem about the seaside, perhaps consisting of brief 'snapshot' verses each on one aspect of the day, e.g. waves, sand, shells, crabs, ice-cream, sandcastles, etc. (the children can brainstorm these first);
- an invented funny story about a family's trip to the seaside during which everything that can go wrong does.

Further reading
- Ask a group of children to find more poems about the sea and give them a opportunity to share them with the class.

© 1993 Folens Ltd.

First Visit to the Seaside

I
The new day
Flooded the green bay
In a slow explosion of blue
Sky and silver sand and shimmering sea.
Boots in hand, I paddled the brilliancy
Of rippled wavelets that withdrew,
Sucking my splay grey
Feet in play.

II
It was magic - the brightness of the air,
the green bay and wide arc of the sea,
with the rock-pools reflecting my stare
and a maze of wind-sculpted sand-dunes where
slum streets and the Quayside should be.

It was music - not only the sound
of the busker outside the pub door
and the band on the pier, but the pounding
of waves, the loud kids all around,
the gulls screaming shrill on the shore.

It was magic and music and motion -
there were yachts sweeping smooth in the bay
and black steamers white-plumed in mid-ocean;
and ice-cream, candy-floss and commotion
as the Switchback got under way.

III
The spent day
Drained from beach and bay
Green and silver and shimmering blue.
On prom and pier, arcade and b. & b.
The looped lights dimly glowed. And I could see
Stars winking at me, glimmering through
The sky's moth-eaten grey
As if in play.

Raymond Wilson

- Work in pairs. Divide a sheet of paper into three columns. Head the first one, <u>What the poet saw</u>. Head the second one, <u>What the poet heard</u>. Head the third one, <u>What the poet did</u>. Using only what you can read in the poem, make a list in each column.
- Make a seaside postcard. On one side make a picture of the seaside as described in the poem. On the other, pretend you are the poet writing a postcard to a friend or relative. Write a message, put the address (you can make it up) and draw a stamp.

Four Children, One Being ... - Ideas Page

Into the poem

Discussion: exploring a mystery

- Explore the meaning of this rather enigmatic poem with a series of questions:
  - Why did the first child cry?
  - Why did the second child run away?
  - Why did the third child stay?
  - Why didn't the fourth child see anything?
- It contains a mystery which is hinted at in the title of the poem. Move the discussion on to this mystery, beginning it with the question: 'What do you think the author is trying to tell us in the poem's mysterious title?'
- List the possible solutions that the children come up with, then as a group evaluate them to see which is the most satisfactory.

Techniques of poetry

- Point out that this is a good example of the free verse form - its flexibility is ideal for the conversational and personal nature of the poem. There is some rhyme but no heightened rhythm.
- It also demonstrates that poems can often have character parts like plays, more usually one voice but in this case four.
- One further point: in the poem the author makes frequent use of the dash. Ask the children to think about the effect these dashes have on the way we read the poem.

Tape it

- Get the children to tape some of the interviews scripted for the activity on the pupil's page.
- This can be played to others who have read the poem but not done the activity.
- Other children might want to role-play the Being being interviewed on tape without any prior scripting.

Taking it further

Poetry writing

- Encourage the children to write a verse similar to that in the poem in which they meet a Being.
- It should contain some description of the Being but more importantly it should indicate how the child felt and thought about it.
- Several of these verses could be put together to form new poems with the same title as the one given, using an adaptation of the last verse in each.

Writing: opinions

- There have long been arguments about the possibility of a parallel civilisation existing somewhere on another planet - it is the stuff of science fiction. Ask the children to discuss the matter then write a personal piece around these three statements:
  - Why I think there is/is not life on another planet.
  - If there is life on another planet, this is the form I think it will take on at least one planet.
  - If I met one of these life-forms, this is what would happen.

Writing: a news report

- Ask the children to imagine how the sighting of a Being - perhaps as described in one of the poem's verses - would be reported in the newspapers.
- Discuss likely headlines and the kind of language that would be used. Talk about how the report would be sequenced and how quotes from those involved would be used. (If the children are not familiar with this kind of writing, select some suitable articles from the press, copy them and discuss the genre with the children).

Art

- The children could select one of the first three verses to illustrate. Only a few clues are given to the appearance of the Being and none for the look of the ship, so this will provide plenty of scope for individual imagination.

A board game

- Pairs or small groups could devise a board game called The Space Journey.
- The project need not end here. Children could not only design the board but also write the rules to go with it and advertise it for sale.

Resources

Cambridge University Press publish two collections of poetry for more than one voice.
Brown, R. *The Midnight Party* (for younger juniors)
Whisked Away (for older juniors)

© 1993 Folens Ltd.

Four Children, One Being ...

In this poem, each verse is a different voice.

The small ship
Came down in the garden
Hardly disturbing the night.
The Being stepped out
As it landed,
Walking upright.
Its fur was like frost
In the moonshine
Sparkling with light.
It was as tall as I
No more -
It looked into my eyes
And knew me sure as sure.
I wanted to show that I liked it,
I wanted to smile -
I tried -
But it set no store
By anything I knew -
I cried ...

No No!
The ship was huge -
The Alien too
But it had no form -
Like fog it was
You could see right through
Eyes it had, I think,
That floated round inside it
Like diamonds they were,
Faceted and prism'd
That surely denied it
Any sight as we see,
The coldness of it
Was space grown
It wasn't anything that could be known
Or could know me
It turned the colour of things to grey
I was terrified -
I ran away.

Not at all!
The ship was small
But did not touch the ground.
The thing rolled out sounding laughter
And bounced around.
It shot out a sort of hand
And showed me in the palm
Stars and planets wheeling.
I thought it meant no harm
Though it whirled around and round me,
Dizzied me and sent me reeling -
I thought it was playing.
It showed me toys and treasure and keys,
Come - come with these, it said,
In no voice that I heard
But I saw that it shrank
From touching trees
And I said, without word -
I'm staying.

I was watching from the window.
What made you act so weird?
Why did you cry
And run
And stare
As though you saw something you feared?
Were you playing a game?
Or did something give you a stare?
I watched from the window
All the time -
And I saw nothing there.

Julie Holder

  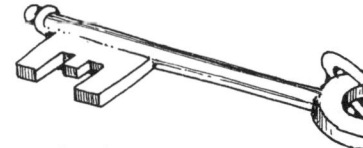

Things To Do

- In pairs, write a list of questions you would like to ask the space Being. Leave a space between each question for an answer. Then pass your questions to another pair who have done the same. Ask them to pretend to be the space Being and to try and answer your questions. Do the same with theirs. Then get together to share what you have written.

Into the poem

Techniques of poetry

- It is worth pointing out that this poem has been translated into a kind of free verse, i.e. having no regular metre of rhyme, although the conventional use of capitals at the beginning of each line gives the poem an appropriate formality.
- The poem is rich in examples of metaphor. Point out some examples and then ask the children to find some more. E.g.
  'You are, bird, the snowdrift's glow.'
  'You are a master fisher'
  'Your fishing rod ... Is your long and lovely neck'
  all of the last seven lines.
- Metaphor is sometimes difficult for younger children to grasp. Ask them questions firstly about literal language:
  - Would a swan really be wearing a white robe? Is this what the poet means? Follow this by investigating what the metaphor adds to the description of the poem - its effect.
- Throughout the poem there are references to the swan's 'nobility', e.g. 'angelic hue', 'Lordship', 'master fisher', 'noble', 'keeper of the oval lake', 'the moon among bird', 'a cock of heaven'. Having pointed this out to the group, you could ask the children the following:
  - 'Why did the poet include all these things?'
  - 'If we were writing a poem about a swan today, what images of "nobility" or specialness might we use instead?'

The Swan - Ideas Page

Taking it further

Genres

- Find a factual description of a swan from an information book. Give copies of it alongside the poem to the group and ask them to think about the essential differences between the two descriptions.
- This will help illustrate the different functions and approaches of two genres apparently doing the same descriptive job.

Word play: talking and writing

- Some swans are black. Ask the group to substitute all references to white in the poem with comparable ones for black.
- Next, change the animal in the poem to a crocodile and then make all further references appropriate to it but keeping as close as possible to the original wording, e.g.

'Crocodile, in your beautiful lake,
As green-robed as a cactus,
You are, reptile, the lakebed's crust,
Devil hued, flat-footed ...'

Poetry writing

- The poem uses the convention of addressing its subject directly, as if speaking to it. In particular, the phrase 'You are ...' is used several times. This can be used to help children write a poem which addresses its subject directly and is rich in metaphor. Ask them to choose a subject, and then begin each line with the phrase 'You are ... ', completing it with a metaphor.

SNAIL
You are a miniature dinosaur.
You are a night traveller.
You are a maker of silver roads.
You are a rock climber.
You are a slow slider ...

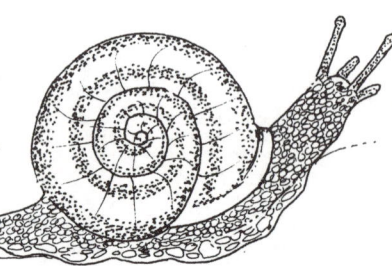

Annotate the poem

- Groups of two or three children can be encouraged to write comments and questions around the poem on the sheet itself, which they discuss with the class later. This is a good way of getting children to tackle the problems of poetry in an anxiety-free atmosphere.

Simile

- Find examples of simile in the poem. Remind children that a simile is a comparison between two things using the words like or as.
- Contrast these with the use of metaphor. What is the difference between them?
- Write poems which consist of only similes. Using opposites provides a reliable structure:

As swift as a cheetah, as slow as a slug ...
As grand as a Queen, as poor as a slave ...

© 1993 Folens Ltd.

The Swan

Swan, on your beautiful lake,
As white-robed as an abbot,
You are, bird, the snowdrift's glow,
Angelic hue, round-footed.
Most solemn are your movements.
Handsome you are in your youth.
God has granted you for life
Lordship of Lake Yfaddon.

Two skills keep you from drowning,
Splendid gifts granted to you:
You are a master fisher,
Look at your skill on the lake,
And you are able to fly
Far above the high hilltop,
Glancing down, noble white bird,
To survey the earth's surface,
Scanning the lake-floor below,
Harvesting shoals like snowflakes.
You ride the waves superbly
To waylay fish from the deep.
Your fishing rod, fair creature,
Is your long and lovely neck,
Keeper of the oval lake,
Breast the colour of seafoam.
You gleam on rippling water
In a crystal-coloured shirt,
A doublet, thousand lillies,
A splendid waistcoat, you wear,
A jacket of white roses,
With wind flowers for a gown.
You are a moon among birds,
White-cloaked, a cock of heaven.

Anon.

Things To Do

- Make a list of all the different ways the poet expresses the swan's whiteness. Then put them in order, beginning with the one you like best.

- Draw a large outline of a swan. Choose some words, phrases or lines from the poem and write them either in or around the swan. You can add words and phrases of your own if you wish.

Between the Lines - Ideas Page

Into the poem

This is a modern American poem which attacks the traditional role of the princess in fairy tales in order to make a feminist point. It is a point of view which needs exploring with children.

Discussion
- Talk about why the poet thinks the princesses in traditional fairy tales are not satisfied with their lives.
- Talk about the traditional role of princes in fairy tales. Why do they feel they have to do the rather absurd things the poet pokes fun of? How do they feel about it?
- Then discuss the relevance of this poem to ordinary people's lives today.
  To what extent are the traditional roles still prevalent in the children's own homes? Is there scope for change?

Techniques of poetry
- This is a good example of a poem in free verse form. Most poetry for children uses formal structures of rhythm, rhyme and verse, so it is worth drawing the children's attention to the free verse form of this poem. In order to mirror the poet's attempt to make sense of unfamiliar territory, free verse dispenses with a regular rhythmic beat in each line, the line breaks are more flexible, and in this example there are no verses or rhyme. It is much closer to spoken language. Highlight these points with the children, then ask them to compare the poem with another that uses a rhyming verse form: what are the essential differences?

Taking it further

Role play
- Put the children into pairs. One role plays the princess in the poem, the other the prince. They agree that their roles need to change if they are to lead more rounded and satisfying lives. Together they work out a new pattern to their lives. But what pattern? In role play the children should work this out then make a note of the main points to share with the rest of the class or group.

Writing
- Encourage the children to write a fairy story in which the traditional roles of the prince and princess or king or queen are reversed or at least changed. To stimulate this, read one or two examples taken from the list given opposite.

Resources

- There is a growing collection of fiction for children which portrays girls and women in non-traditional roles, often in an amusing and punchy way. You can take the issues raised in the poem further by collecting as many of these books as you can, making a display of them, reading some to the class, discussing them and encouraging the children to read them. To get you started, here are some titles:

  BROWN, Anthony: *Piggybook*, Anderson 1986 (a picture book)
  COLE, Babette: *Princess Smartypants*, Viking (a picture book)
  CORBALIS, Judy: *The Wrestling Princess and other stories*, Deutsch 1986 (short stories and poems)
  IMPEY, Rose: *Who's a Clever Girl, Then?* Heinemann Banana Books 1986 (a short novel for newly independent readers)
  KEMP, Gene: *The Turbulent Term of Tyke Tiler*, Puffin 1979 (a novel)
  LURIE, Alison: *Clever Gretchen and Other Forgotten Heroines*, Heinemann (folk tales)
  PAOLA, Tomi de: *Oliver Button is a Sissy*, Methuen 1981 (a picture book)
  WILLIAMS, Jay: *The Practical Princess and Other Stories*, Hippo Books 1983

© 1993 Folens Ltd.

Between the Lines

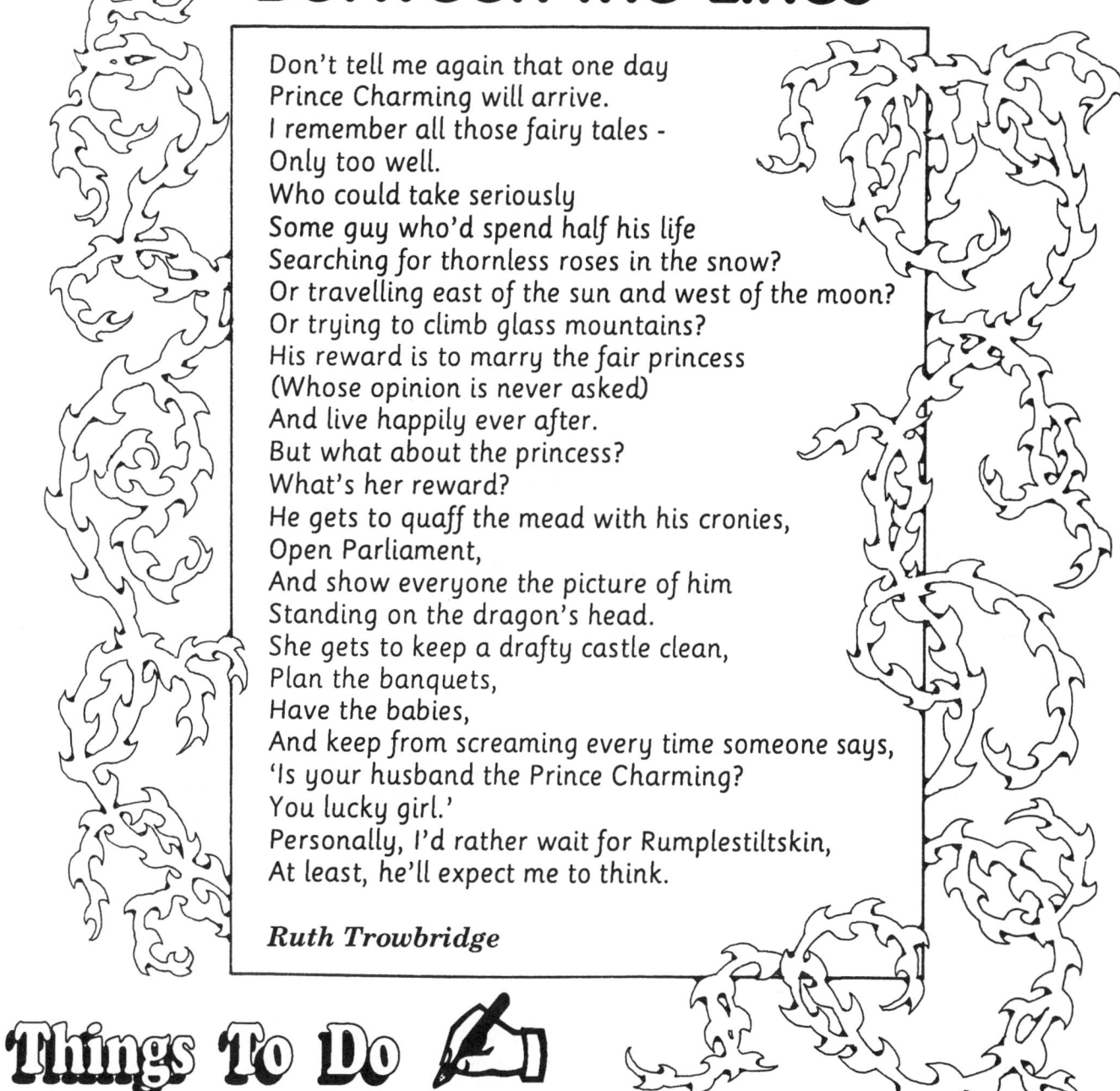

Don't tell me again that one day
Prince Charming will arrive.
I remember all those fairy tales -
Only too well.
Who could take seriously
Some guy who'd spend half his life
Searching for thornless roses in the snow?
Or travelling east of the sun and west of the moon?
Or trying to climb glass mountains?
His reward is to marry the fair princess
(Whose opinion is never asked)
And live happily ever after.
But what about the princess?
What's her reward?
He gets to quaff the mead with his cronies,
Open Parliament,
And show everyone the picture of him
Standing on the dragon's head.
She gets to keep a drafty castle clean,
Plan the banquets,
Have the babies,
And keep from screaming every time someone says,
'Is your husband the Prince Charming?
You lucky girl.'
Personally, I'd rather wait for Rumplestiltskin,
At least, he'll expect me to think.

Ruth Trowbridge

Things To Do

- The poet is complaining about the roles of Prince and Princess, King and Queen in fairy tales. Look through a few books of fairy tales and see whether her complaint is a fair one.
- Following this, make two lists of fairy tales. One will be about Princesses as described in the second half of the poem. The other will be about Princesses who are freer and have more power. Does this prove that the poet is right?
- In your group or pair, retell the story of Rumpelstiltskin. If you do not know the story, see if you can find it in a book of folk or fairy tales, or ask someone who does know it to retell it to you. Then talk about the last two lines of the poem: what do they mean?

Victoria 1837 - Ideas Page

Into the poem

Research
- This poem has been chosen more for its didactic intentions than for its poetic qualities. Victorian studies are now a popular subject for history and a poem which contains so many references to Victorian notables is a welcome introduction for the children to the subject and provides a way into basic research.
- You will need to make sure that each group (mixed ability) in the quiz set at the end of the poem, has a collection of reference books at the right level which contain the answers they will be looking for. If some references are missing, note these and give them to the children to start them off.
- It would be useful, too, to find a book on the history of stamps in this country, so that you could show how the penny and halfpenny changed colour - something that the poem makes much of.

Vocabulary and meaning
- Some of the language and concepts of this poem are a little dated. Before you begin the research and quiz work, ask children to underline or highlight any words and phrases in the poem they would like to have explained. If you are not going to follow up with the quiz, then the references to the famous people will need to be written out on the board by you and explained.

Taking it further

Research profiles
- Each pair of children could research one of the notables mentioned in the poem, writing a summary of what they have discovered. These could be displayed around the poem on a pinboard for other children to read.

Art
- The poem refers to contemporary stamps. Ask the children to select one of the famous people featured in the poem and design a stamp for that person to commemorate their lives or main achievement.
- If more than one child does the same person then a 'post office selection committee' can be set up to decide which of the designs would be the one finally chosen for 'printing'.

Performance
- Groups of children can be given a verse of the poem to study. Two children read out the verse while the other members of the group mime suitable actions. Put all the work on the verses together as a performance.

Artefacts
- Use the poem as an opportunity to make a collection of artefacts linked to the poem:
  - old photographs
  - old stamp album
  - novels of Charles Dickens
  - a menu of a Victorian meal
  - Tennyson's poems.

  Discuss what can be learned or deduced about the period from the objects.

Phraseology
- A reading of the poem will make the children aware of the fact that several phrases are no longer used, or sound 'old-fashioned'. In other words, language is constantly changing:
  - happy days long fled
  - powers in the land.
- Discuss with the children what these mean and make a list of how we would communicate such ideas today.

© 1993 Folens Ltd.

Victoria 1837

In 1932 Eleanor and Herbert Farjeon published a book of rhymes called Kings and Queens. This one is about Victoria who reigned from 1819 to 1901.

Victoria, Victoria,
Was England's pride and joy
When grandma was a baby
And grandpa was a boy,
And they can still remember
The happy days long fled,
When the penny stamp was purple
And the ha'penny stamp was red.

Then Salisbury and Gladstone
Were powers in the land,
And Dickens was an idol,
And the Albert Hall was grand;
And hostesses resorted
To Gunter's for a spread,
When the penny stamp was purple
And the ha'penny was red.

Then saucy Nellie Farren
Was billed upon the boards,
And Grace sat in a growler
And bundled down to Lords,
And every one repeated
What Mr Whistler said,
When the penny stamp was purple
And the ha'penny was red.

Then Wolsey or whoever
Went forth to fight our foes
Was honoured by Lord Tennyson
As well as by Tussaud's,
And Watts and Ouida were alive
And Darwin wasn't dead,
When the penny stamp was purple
And the ha'penny stamp was red.

Now the penny stamp is scarlet
And the ha'penny stamp is green - *
How different from the days when Queen
Victoria was queen.
The far-off days when Grandpa
And Grandmamma were wed,
And the penny stamp was purple
And the ha'penny stamp was red.

*Till AD 1951
This chronicle rang true -
Then the ha'penny stamp turned orange
And the penny stamp turned blue.*

*Now the ha'penny stamp is blue
And the penny stamp maroon
But that is all too likely
To be altered very soon.*

Eleanor and Herbert Farjeon

Things To Do

Get into teams of three or four. Within the time set by your teacher, you get a point every time you find out who in the poem was the following:

an actress
a cricketer
two painters
two novelists
a poet
two prime ministers
a naturalist
a field marshal

You get a point every time you find out what these are:

an idol
the Albert Hall
Gunter's
billed upon the boards
a growler
Lords
Tussaud's

Wee Jouky Daidles - Ideas Page

Into the poem

Dialect

- This is a good example of written dialect, made more accessible by its rhyming, rhythmic context. It was probably written in the 19th century, and Scottish dialect speakers may want to examine it for signs of language change over time.
- The challenge for those without knowledge of Scottish dialect is twofold: meaning and pronunciation. Both are problem-solving opportunities worth presenting to children - who can become quite fascinated by dialect. If you are working with a group, it is probably best to begin by talking about varieties in the national accent (word pronunciation) and dialect (word pronunciation with the addition of words and grammar peculiar to the dialect). How many children in the class, for example, have an accent or a dialect different to the majority? What are its geographical roots? Then explain that there are many Scottish dialects, of which this purports to be one.
- Next, try reading it aloud to the group yourself (it is worth practising beforehand). Then encourage the whole group to read it together. Point out that there are two main clues to pronunciation: punctuation and spelling. Explore the frequent use of the apostrophe used to indicate the dropping of sounds, e.g. **Toddlin'**, **Makin'**.
- Once you have had fun doing this, take each verse and discuss any problems of meaning and pronunciation. The children are then in a position to do the two things suggested on the pupil sheet.
- With the group, compile a **glossary** of words in dialect. Begin by asking pairs to underline dialect words, giving them one or two verses each to work on. Discuss meanings before you agree on a definition. There may, of course, be some meanings that elude the group.

Taking it further

Write a dialogue

- The voice of the poem is almost certainly Jouky's mother. Her father is only mentioned once. Talk with the children about the mother's attitude to Jouky's misbehaviour. Then ask them to write a dialogue between Jouky's parents, with the father calling for greater control of the child.

Role-play an interview

- Ask the children to work in pairs. One of them is an indulgent aunt to Jouky, the other is Jouky herself. The aunt is asking Jouky why she did the various things described in the poem, e.g. Why did you break the dishes, Jouky? Why did you allow yourself to get soaked in the river? etc. The pupil playing Jouky should try and think of answers the girl might give herself.

Mime

- Use the poem as a source of mime for the whole class in the hall. The children act out Jouky's deeds. This can either be done with you reading the poem aloud and the children responding individually. Or you can divide the class into small groups, one child in each reading the poem aloud and pausing for actions, while the rest respond with mime. The one can, of course, follow the other.

Poems in dialect

- This poem could well stimulate an interest in poems written in dialect. See if you can find some other examples of dialect poetry and make a display of them. Share them in the way you normally share poems in class.

Writing poems in dialect

- There is no reason why, if the children have the skills, they should not have a go at writing poems in dialect themselves. Some examples of children writing poems in dialect can be found in some of Cadbury's collection of children's poetry, published in paperback annually by Beaver Books.

© 1993 Folens Ltd.

Wee Jouky Daidles

Here is an old Scottish poem about a lively and mischievous little girl called Jouky Daidles. It is written in a Scottish dialect. This may make it hard to read at first. Try reading it aloud with a friend.

Wee Jouky Daidles,
Toddlin' out an' in:
Oh, but she's a cuttie,
Makin' sic a din!
She sae fon' o' mischief,
An' minds na what I say:
My verra heart gangs loup, loup,
Fifty times a day!

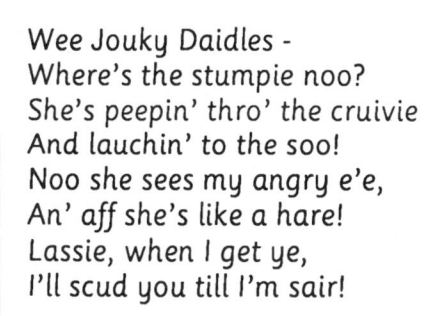

Wee Jouky Daidles -
Where's the stumpie noo?
She's peepin' thro' the cruivie
And lauchin' to the soo!
Noo she sees my angry e'e,
An' aff she's like a hare!
Lassie, when I get ye,
I'll scud you till I'm sair!

Wee Jouky Daidles -
Noo she's breakin' dishes -
Noo she's soak it i' the burn,
Catchin' little fishes -
Noo she's i' the barn-yard,
Playin' w' the fowls;
Feedin' them wi' butter-bakes,
Snaps, an' sugar-bools.

Wee Jouky Daidles -
Oh, my heart, it's broke!
She's torn my braw new wincey
To make a dolly's frock -
There's the goblet oure the fire!
The jaud! she weel may rin!
Not a tattic ready yet,
An' faither comin' in!

Wee Jouky Daidles -
Paidlin' i' the shower -
There she's at the windy!
Haud her or she's oure!
Noo she's slippit frae my sicht;
Where's the wean at last?
In the byre amang the kye,
Sleepin' soun' an' fast!

Wee Jouky Daidles -
For a' ye gi' me pain,
Ye're aye my darlin' tottie yet -
My ain wee wean!
Ah! gin I'm spared to ither days -
Oh, may they come to pass! -
I'll see my bonnie bairnie
A braw, braw lass!

James Smith

Things To Do

- When you have worked out roughly what is happening in this poem, make a list of all the mischievous things Jouky gets up to. Then see if you can put them in order, starting with the naughtiest deed and ending with the least naughtiest.
- Choose one of the verses and copy it in your best writing on one side of a folded sheet of paper. On the other make a careful illustration of the verse.

© 1993 Folens Ltd.   This page may be photocopied for classroom use only

Kubla Khan - Ideas Page

Into the poem

First encounter
- The visual splendour presented by this poem, and its hypnotic sonority and rhythm, will capture the children's attention before they will fully comprehend much of its meaning. So before you go on to look at individual words, ask the children to describe the pictures the poem creates in their minds. Then say it aloud together, as in choral speaking, so that the poem begins to become familiar.

Vocabulary
- Next, explain the activity described on the pupil's page. Make sure you have a few good dictionaries available to the group. You could demonstrate the task by saying that you were not sure yourself what 'sinuous rills' referred to and checked its meaning in the dictionary. (**Sinuous**: *with many curves, serpentine, undulating.* **Rill**: *small stream, rivulet*). Once the children have compiled their glossary and tried to use words from it as alternatives to those in the poem, you can talk about synonyms and what governs the poet's precise choice of words.

Art
- Xanadu is a province of China. The extracts selected here are very visual; the poem is in essence a description. One way, therefore, of creating a good understanding of the poem in detail is to ask the children to draw an outline of a picture of the walled pleasure garden. Each of the key elements would need to be discussed first and where they have to be placed in relation to each other: the pleasure-dome (what does it look like?); the river Alph; the sea; walls and towers; the gardens; trees and forests; caverns; the fountain. Once the outlines have been finalised, colour could be added.

Taking it further

The pleasure-dome
- The pleasure-dome is not described and its nature is not given. So here there is scope for the children's imagination. Through a sharing of ideas, work out what the dome might look like, be made of, and more importantly, what it would have inside it. Then bring the idea up-to-date and ask pairs or small groups to create a large cross-section drawing of what a modern Kubla Khan might want his pleasure-dome to look like and what might be in it.

The nature of writing poetry
- This poem is famous for being unfinished. Discuss the use of the three dots at the end of the passage. What do they mean?
- Coleridge claimed that 'the person from Porlock' interrupted the inspired flow and effectively killed its completion. But another poet, Stevie Smith, was sceptical about this and in a poem called **Thoughts about the Person from Porlock** humorously speculated:

    *... the truth is I think that he was already stuck
    With Kubla Khan ...*

- Share this thought with the group and ask them to discuss whether they think Smith is being fair. This could lead on to a discussion of where ideas come from in writing and what the best conditions are for carrying them out.

Poetry writing
- Once the children are thoroughly familiar with the poem's imagery by drawing pictures of what the poet is describing, ask them to write a free verse poem describing what the Kubla Khan's pleasure garden looks like:
    - in the depths of a snowy winter
    - in the early Spring
    - in Autumn.

© 1993 Folens Ltd.

Kubla Khan

Here's part of a famous poem written in 1797. The story goes that Coleridge awoke one morning with the poem already formed in his head. He began to write it but was interrupted by a visitor, 'a person from Porlock'. When he returned to the poem he found that it had vanished from his memory.

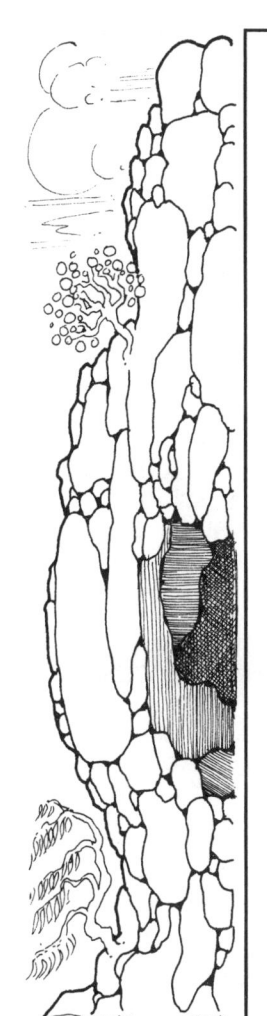

> In Xanadu did Kubla Khan
> A stately pleasure-dome decree:
> Where Alph, the sacred river, ran
> Through caverns measureless to man
>   Down to a sunless sea.
> So twice five miles of fertile ground
> With walls and towers were girdled round:
> And here were gardens bright with sinuous rills,
> Where blossomed many an incense-bearing tree;
> And here were forests ancient as the hills,
> Enfolding sunny spots of greenery ...
>
> Five miles meandering with a mazy motion
> Through wood and dale the sacred river ran,
> Then reached the caverns measureless to man,
> And sank in tumult to a lifeless ocean ...
>
>   The shadow of the dome of pleasure
>   Floated midway on the waves;
>   Where was heard the mingled measure
>   From the fountain and the caves.
> It was a miracle of rare device,
> A sunny pleasure-dome with caves of ice! ...
>
> **Samuel Taylor Coleridge**

Things To Do

- This poem was written nearly 200 years ago so there are words in it you may find unfamiliar. In your group, underline these words and talk about what they might mean. Then check their meaning in a large dictionary. Write a glossary of the words.

- When your glossary is complete, see what happens when you try and replace some of the words you underlined with others from your glossary. What is gained? What is lost? Discuss this with a partner.

Grammar in a Nutshell - Ideas Page

Into the poem

A cautionary note
- This is a rhyme - or a rhyming mnemonic - which has been in existence for a long time. It appears, for example, in E. V. Lucas's **Another Book of Verses for Children** which was published in 1907. It goes in and out of fashion regularly, partly reflecting contemporary attitudes to the teaching of grammar, partly because it's recognised that it is somewhat simplistic in its approach to the subject. For example, it gives the impression that words belong to only one category, whereas words change their grammatical function according to the way they are used within the sentence. Thus 'school' in the rhyme is correctly identified as a noun, but when it is used thus - 'the school garden' - it becomes an adjective. My dictionary tells me that the word 'as' can be an adverb, a conjunction or a preposition.
- We need to be aware of the differences between grammar in its widest sense and sentence grammar as outlined in this poem.
- It is important, then, that this rhyme is not left to stand on its own. It needs to be used within the context of grammar teaching, preferably as a reinforcement, and it's limitations need to be highlighted in the way I illustrated above. Having said that, it is a useful mnemonic and worth encouraging children to learn it.

Spot the function
- Once you have shared and discussed the rhyme in the group, you can begin to set work which tests whether its information can be applied. Give a copy of another poem from this book to each child or pair (one they are already familiar with). Choose one of the verses from the grammar rhyme and say that together you are going to test whether it is true. Ask the children to circle or underline any examples of that grammatical function in the poem, using a coloured pencil. Compare results, and if the approach is reasonably successful, try it with another part of speech, using a different coloured pencil. It is something that can be returned to several times.

Taking it further

Quick grammar games
- Once various parts of speech are understood, you can set children some quick grammar games, e.g.
Adjectives: how many adjectives can you use to describe a snail crawling up a window?
Pronouns: read aloud from your reading book but replace all pronouns with the appropriate noun or proper noun.
Verbs: how many verbs for movement can you write in five minutes?
Preposition: a fox is going on a journey - how many prepositions can be used to describe the journey? e.g. **Out** of the burrow, **Over** the leaves, **Under** the gate.
Classification: each child or pair gathers a list of 15-20 favourite words from their classmates and then try to classify them into grammatical functions using the rhyme as a reference. Results can be compared to find which is the favourite part of speech.

Implicit knowledge about language
- Children have a vast and complex **implicit** knowledge of grammatical rules developed through learning to speak and refined through reading and writing. Give the children some grammatically jumbled sentences and ask them to unscramble them. Then you ask a crucial follow-up question: *'You knew what the right order of words should be - but **how** did you know?'*
- Examine the issues raised by the poem opposite.

Resources

I take it you already know
Of tough and bough and cough and dough?
Others may stumble, but not you
On hiccough, through, laugh and though?
I write in case you wish perhaps
To learn of less familiar traps:
Beware of heard, a dreadful word
That looks like beard and sounds like bird.
And dead: it's said like bed not bead;
For goodness sake, don't call it 'deed'!
Watch out for me at and great and threat
(They rhyme with suite and straight and debt).
A moth is not a moth in mother,
Nor both in bother, or broth in brother ...
A dreadful language? Man alive,
I'd mastered it when I was five!

© 1993 Folens Ltd.

Grammar in a Nutshell

Sentences are made up of different kinds of words. For example, the noun, adjective, pronoun, verb and so on. These different kinds of words are often called <u>parts of speech</u>. This old rhyme was once used by generations of children to remind them about parts of speech.

> I
> Three little words you often see
> Are articles - <u>a</u>, <u>an</u> and <u>the</u>
> II
> A noun's the name of anything,
> As <u>school</u> or <u>garden</u>, <u>hoop</u> or <u>swing</u>.
> III
> Adjectives, the kind of noun,
> As <u>great</u>, <u>small</u>, <u>pretty</u>, <u>white</u>, or <u>brown</u>.
> IV
> Instead of nouns the pronouns stand -
> <u>Her</u> head, <u>his</u> face, <u>your</u> arm, <u>my</u> hand.
> V
> Verbs tell something to be done -
> To <u>read</u>, <u>count</u>, <u>laugh</u>, <u>sing</u>, <u>jump</u>, or <u>run</u>.
> VI
> How things are done the adverbs tell,
> As <u>slowly</u>, <u>quickly</u>, <u>ill</u>, or <u>well</u>.
> VII
> Conjunctions join the words together,
> As men <u>and</u> women, wind <u>or</u> weather.
> VIII
> The preposition stands before
> A noun, as <u>in</u> or <u>through</u> a door.
> IX
> The interjection shows surprise,
> As <u>oh! how pretty! ah! how wise!</u>
> X
> The whole are called nine parts of speech,
> Which reading, writing, speaking teach.
>
> **Anon**

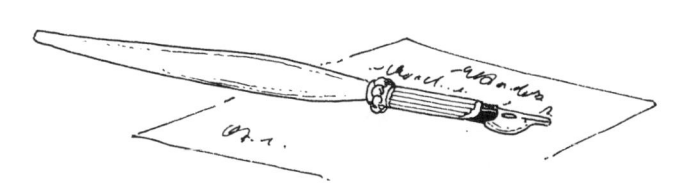

Things To Do

- In pairs, read the rhyme aloud. One of you reads the ordinary print, the other the print underlined. Then change over and do it again. Begin to learn the rhyme off by heart - you may find it useful.

- Talk with a partner or in your group about each verse. Each verse has some examples of the parts of speech and these are underlined. See if you can think of a few more examples for each verse and write them down.

Eight ways to help ...

There are hundreds of ideas in this book to enable you to develop and extend the photocopiable pages. Here are just eight ways to help you make the most of the Ideas Bank series.

1. Photocopy a page, paste on to card and laminate/cover with sticky-backed plastic to use with groups. Children can now write on the pages using water-based pens and this can be washed off.

2. Photocopy on to both sides of the paper. Put another useful activity on the back. Develop a simple filing system so others can find relevant sheets and do not duplicate them again.

3. Save the sheets - if the children do not have to cut them up as a part of the activity - and re-use. Label the sets, and keep them safely in files.

4. Make the most of group work. Children working in small groups need one sheet to discuss between them.

5. Put the sheets inside clear plastic wallets. This means the sheets are easily stored in a binder and will last longer. Children's writing can again be wiped away.

6. Use as an ideas page for yourself. Discuss issues with the class and get children to produce artwork and writing.

7. Make an overhead transparency of the page. You and your colleagues can now use the idea time and time again.

8. Ask yourself, 'Does every child in this class/group need to deal with/work through this photocopiable sheet?' If not, don't photocopy it!

© 1993 Folens Ltd.